Vwilson

Editor
Cristina Krysinski, M. Ed.

Editor in Chief
Karen J. Goldfluss, M.S. Ed.

Creative Director
Sarah M. Fournier

Cover Artist
Barbara Lorseyedi

Art Coordinator
Renée Mc Elwee

Imaging
Amanda R. Harter

Publisher
Mary D. Smith, M.S. Ed.

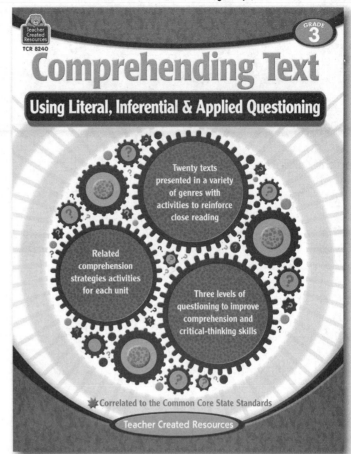

GRADE 3

Comprehending Text
Using Literal, Inferential & Applied Questioning

Twenty texts presented in a variety of genres with activities to reinforce close reading

Related comprehension strategies activities for each unit

Three levels of questioning to improve comprehension and critical-thinking skills

★ Correlated to the Common Core State Standards

Teacher Created Resources

CORRELATED TO COMMON CORE STANDARDS

For correlations to the Common Core State Standards, see page 109 of this book or visit *http://www.teachercreated.com/standards*.

The classroom teacher may reproduce the materials in this book and/or CD for use in a single classroom only. The reproduction of any part of this book and/or CD for other classrooms or for an entire school or school system is strictly prohibited. No part of this publication may be transmitted or recorded in any form without written permission from the publisher with the exception of electronic material, which may be stored on the purchaser's computer only.

Teacher Created Resources
6421 Industry Way
Westminster, CA 92683
www.teachercreated

ISBN: 978-1-4206-82

© 2015 Teacher Created
Made in U.S.A.

D1402539

Teacher Created Resources

Table of Contents

Introduction

Twenty different texts from a variety of genres are included in this reading comprehension resource. These may include humor, fantasy, myth/legend, folktale, mystery, adventure, suspense, fairy tale, play, fable, science fiction, poetry, and informational/nonfiction texts, such as a timetable, letter, report, procedure, poster, map, program, book cover, and cartoon.

Three levels of questions are used to indicate the reader's comprehension of each text.

One or more particular comprehension strategies have been chosen for practice with each text.

Each unit is five pages long and consists of the following resources and strategies:

- teacher information: includes the answer key and extension suggestions
- text page: text is presented on one full page
- activity page 1:   covers literal and inferential questions
- activity page 2:   covers applied questions
- applying strategies: focuses on a chosen comprehension strategy/strategies

Teacher Information

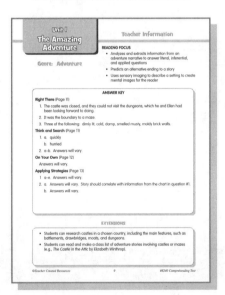

- **Reading Focus** states the comprehension skill emphasis for the unit.
- **Genre** is clearly indicated.
- **Answer Key** is provided. For certain questions, answers will vary, but suggested answers are given.
- **Extension Activities** suggest other authors or book titles. Other literacy activities relating to the text are suggested.

Text Page

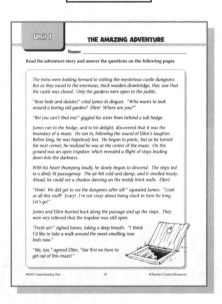

- The title of the text is provided.
- Statement is included in regard to the genre.
- Text is presented on a full page.

Activity Page 1

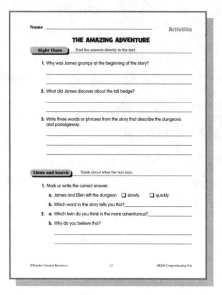

Activity Page 2

- **Right There** consists of literal questions.

- **Think and Search** consists of inferential questions.

- **On Your Own** consists of applied questions.

Applying Strategies

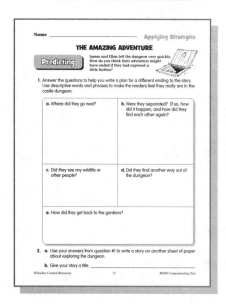

- Comprehension strategy focus is clearly labeled.

- Activities provide opportunities to utilize the particular strategy.

Types of Questions

Students are given **three types of questions** (all grouped accordingly) to assess their comprehension of a particular text in each genre:

- **Literal questions (Right There)** are questions for which answers can be found directly in the text.

- **Inferential questions (Think and Search)** are questions for which answers are implied in the text and require the reader to think a bit more deeply about what he or she has just read.

- **Applied questions (On Your Own)** are questions that require the reader to think even further about the text and incorporate personal experiences and knowledge to answer them.

Answers for literal questions are always given and may be found on the Teacher Information pages. Answers for inferential questions are given when appropriate. Applied questions are best checked by the teacher following, or in conjunction with, a class discussion.

Comprehension Strategies

Several specific comprehension strategies have been selected for practice in this book.

Although specific examples have been selected, often other strategies, such as scanning, are used in conjunction with those indicated, even though they may not be stated. Rarely does a reader use only a single strategy to comprehend a text.

Strategy Definitions

Predicting	Prediction involves the students using illustrations, text, or background knowledge to help them construct meaning. Students might predict what texts could be about, what could happen, or how characters could act or react. Prediction may occur before, during, and after reading, and it can be adjusted during reading.
Making Connections	Students comprehend texts by linking their prior knowledge with the new information from the text. Students may make connections between the text and themselves, between the new text and other texts previously read, and between the text and real-world experiences.
Comparing	This strategy is closely linked to the strategy of making connections. Students make comparisons by thinking more specifically about the similarities and differences between the connections being made.
Sensory Imaging	Sensory imaging involves students utilizing all five senses to create mental images of passages in the text. Students also use their personal experiences to create these images. The images may help students make predictions, form conclusions, interpret information, and remember details.

Strategy Definitions *(cont.)*

Determining Importance/ Identifying Main Idea(s)	The strategy of determining importance is particularly helpful when students try to comprehend informational texts. It involves students determining the important theme or main idea of particular paragraphs or passages.
	As students become effective readers, they will constantly ask themselves what is most important in a phrase, sentence, paragraph, chapter, or whole text. To determine importance, students will need to use a variety of information, such as the purpose for reading, their knowledge of the topic, background experiences and beliefs, and understanding of the text format.
Skimming	Skimming is the strategy of looking quickly through texts to gain a general impression or overview of the content. Readers often use this strategy to quickly assess whether a text, or part of it, will meet their purpose. Because this book deals predominantly with comprehension after reading, skimming has not been included as one of the major strategies.
Scanning	Scanning is the strategy of quickly locating specific details, such as dates, places, or names, or those parts of the text that support a particular point of view. Scanning is often used, but not specifically mentioned, when used in conjunction with other strategies.
Synthesizing/Sequencing	Synthesizing is the strategy that enables students to collate a range of information in relation to the text. Students recall information, order details, and piece information together to make sense of the text. Synthesizing/sequencing helps students to monitor their understanding. Synthesizing involves connecting, comparing, determining importance, posing questions, and creating images.
Summarizing/Paraphrasing	Summarizing involves the processes of recording key ideas, main points, or the most important information from a text. Summarizing or paraphrasing reduces a larger piece of text to the most important details.

Genre Definitions

Fiction and Poetry

Science Fiction   These stories include backgrounds or plots based upon possible technology or inventions, experimental medicine, life in the future, environments drastically changed, alien races, space travel, genetic engineering, dimensional portals, or changed scientific principles. Science fiction encourages readers to suspend some of their disbelief and examine alternate possibilities.

Suspense   Stories of suspense aim to make the reader feel fear, disgust, or uncertainty. Many suspense stories have become classics. These include *Frankenstein* by Mary Shelley, *Dracula* by Bram Stoker, and *Dr. Jekyll and Mr. Hyde* by Robert Louis Stevenson.

Mystery   Stories from this genre focus on the solving of a mystery. Plots of mysteries often revolve around a crime. The hero must solve the mystery, overcoming unknown forces or enemies. Stories about detectives, police, private investigators, amateur sleuths, spies, thrillers, and courtroom dramas usually fall into this genre.

Fable   A fable is a short story that states a moral. Fables often use talking animals or animated objects as the main characters. The interaction of the animals or animated objects reveals general truths about human nature.

Fairy Tale   These tales are usually about elves, dragons, goblins, fairies, or magical beings and are often set in the distant past. Fairy tales usually begin with the phrase "Once upon a time . . ." and end with the words ". . . and they lived happily ever after." Charms, disguises, and talking animals may also appear in fairy tales.

Fantasy   A fantasy may be any text or story removed from reality. Stories may be set in nonexistent worlds, such as an elf kingdom, on another planet, or in alternate versions of the known world. The characters may not be human (dragons, trolls, etc.) or may be humans who interact with non-human characters.

Folktale   Stories that have been passed from one generation to the next by word of mouth rather than by written form are folktales. Folktales may include sayings, superstitions, social rituals, legends, or lore about the weather, animals, or plants.

Play   Plays are specific pieces of drama, usually enacted on a stage by actors dressed in makeup and appropriate costumes.

Adventure   Exciting events and actions feature in these stories. Character development, themes, or symbolism are not as important as the actions or events in an adventure story.

Humor   Humor involves characters or events that promote laughter, pleasure, or humor in the reader.

Genre Definitions (cont.)

Fiction and Poetry (cont.)

Poetry
This genre utilizes rhythmic patterns of language. The patterns include meter (high- and low-stressed syllables), syllabication (the number of syllables in each line), rhyme, alliteration, or a combination of these. Poems often use figurative language.

Myth
A myth explains a belief, practice, or natural phenomenon and usually involves gods, demons, or supernatural beings. A myth does not necessarily have a basis in fact or a natural explanation.

Legend
Legends are told as though the events were actual historical events. Legends may or may not be based on an elaborated version of a historical event. Legends are usually about human beings, although gods may intervene in some way throughout the story.

Nonfiction

Report
Reports are written documents describing the findings of an individual or group. They may take the form of a newspaper report, sports report, or police report, or a report about an animal, person, or object.

Biography
A biography is an account of a person's life written by another person. The biography may be about the life of a celebrity or a historical figure.

Review
A review is a concise summary or critical evaluation of a text, event, object, or phenomenon. A review may present a perspective, argument, or purpose. It offers critical assessment of content, effectiveness, noteworthy features and often ends with a suggestion of audience appreciation.

Letter
These are written conversations sent from one person to another. Letters usually begin with a greeting, contain the information to be related, and conclude with a farewell signed by the sender.

Procedure
Procedures tell how to make or do something. They use clear, concise language and command verbs. A list of materials required to complete the procedure is included, and the instructions are set out in easy-to-follow steps.

Diary
Diary entries contain a description of daily events in a person's life.

Other **informational texts**, such as **timetables**, are excellent sources to teach and assess comprehension skills. Highly visual texts, such as **flow charts**, have been included because they provide the reader with other comprehension cues.

Unit 1
The Amazing Adventure

Genre: Adventure

READING FOCUS

- Analyzes and extracts information from an adventure narrative to answer literal, inferential, and applied questions
- Predicts an alternative ending to a story
- Uses sensory imaging to describe a setting to create mental images for the reader

ANSWER KEY

Right There (Page 11)

1. The castle was closed, and they could not visit the dungeons, which he and Ellen had been looking forward to doing.
2. It was the boundary to a maze.
3. Three of the following: dimly lit, cold, damp, smelled musty, moldy brick walls.

Think and Search (Page 11)

1. a. quickly
   b. hurried
2. a–b. Answers will vary.

On Your Own (Page 12)

Answers will vary.

Applying Strategies (Page 13)

1 a–e. Answers will vary.
2. a. Answers will vary. Story should correlate with information from the chart in question #1.
   b. Answers will vary.

EXTENSIONS

- Students can research castles in a chosen country, including the main features, such as battlements, drawbridges, moats, and dungeons.
- Students can read and make a class list of adventure stories involving castles or mazes (e.g., *The Castle in the Attic* by Elizabeth Winthrop).

Name _____

Read the adventure story and answer the questions on the following pages.

The twins were looking forward to visiting the mysterious castle dungeons. But as they raced to the enormous, thick wooden drawbridge, they saw that the castle was closed. Only the gardens were open to the public.

"Rose beds and daisies!" cried James in disgust. "Who wants to look around a boring old garden? Ellen! Where are you?"

"Bet you can't find me!" giggled his sister from behind a tall hedge.

James ran to the hedge, and to his delight, discovered that it was the boundary of a maze. He ran in, following the sound of Ellen's laughter. Before long, he was hopelessly lost. He began to panic, but as he turned the next corner, he realized he was at the center of the maze. On the ground was an open trapdoor, which revealed a flight of steps leading down into the darkness.

With his heart thumping loudly, he slowly began to descend. The steps led to a dimly lit passageway. The air felt cold and damp, and it smelled musty. Ahead, he could see a shadow dancing on the moldy brick walls. Ellen!

"Wow! We did get to see the dungeons after all!" squealed James. "Look at all this stuff! Scary! I'm not crazy about being stuck in here for long. Let's go!"

James and Ellen hurried back along the passage and up the steps. They were very relieved that the trapdoor was still open.

"Fresh air!" sighed James, taking a deep breath. "I think I'd like to take a walk around the sweet-smelling rose beds now."

"Me, too," agreed Ellen, "but first we have to get out of this maze!"

THE AMAZING ADVENTURE

Right There   Find the answers directly in the text.

1. Why was James grumpy at the beginning of the story?

_____

_____

2. What did James discover about the tall hedge?

_____

_____

3. Write three words or phrases from the story that describe the dungeons and passageway.

_____

_____

_____

Think and Search   Think about what the text says.

1. Mark or write the correct answer.

   a. James and Ellen left the dungeon   ☐ slowly.   ☐ quickly.

   b. Which word in the story tells you this?_____

2. **a.** Which twin do you think is the more adventurous?_____

   b. Why do you believe this?

   _____

   _____

THE AMAZING ADVENTURE

On Your Own   Use what you know about the text and your own experience.

James and Ellen wanted to visit the dungeons, yet when they found them, they did not want to stay very long.

Write words and phrases in the boxes to describe a situation that might be both exciting and a little scary.

Brief description of the situation:

_____

_____

_____

Exciting Part(s)	**Scary Part(s)**
_____	_____
_____	_____
_____	_____
_____	_____
_____	_____
_____	_____
_____	_____
_____	_____
_____	_____

THE AMAZING ADVENTURE

Predicting

James and Ellen left the dungeon very quickly. How do you think their adventure might have ended if they had explored a little further?

1. Answer the questions to help you write a plan for a different ending to the story. Use descriptive words and phrases to make the readers feel they really are in the castle dungeon.

a. Where did they go next?	**b.** Were they separated? If so, how did it happen, and how did they find each other again?
c. Did they see any wildlife or other people?	**d.** Did they find another way out of the dungeon?
e. How did they get back to the gardens?	

2. **a.** Use your answers from question #1 to write a story on another sheet of paper about exploring the dungeon.

   b. Give your story a title. _____

Genre: Science Fiction

READING FOCUS

- Analyzes and extracts information from a science-fiction narrative to answer literal, inferential, and applied questions
- Predicts events to complete a story
- Makes a comparison between characters in a story and himself/herself

ANSWER KEY

Right There (Page 16)

1. True
2. False
3. True
4. True

Think and Search (Page 16)

Answers will vary. Possible answers:

1. everyone was talking about it, so they thought it would be good.
2. magical and able to transport her into another dimension.
3. robbed the Sparkles Jewelers store.
4. do karate/defend herself.

On Your Own (Page 17)

1. Anwers will vary.
2. Drawings will vary.

Applying Strategies (Page 18)

1–2. Answers will vary.

EXTENSIONS

- Other suggested science-fiction titles include the following:
  - *I Was a Third Grade Science Project* by Mary Jane Auch
  - *Akiko on the Planet Smoo* by Mark Crilley
  - *The Transmogrification of Roscoe Wizzle* by David Elliott

Name _____

Read the science-fiction story and answer the questions on the following pages.

It was Saturday morning and Carly was at the video store with her mom to choose some DVDs to rent. It was Carly's eighth birthday, and her mom had allowed her to invite four friends to sleep over at her house to celebrate.

She already knew one DVD she wanted to choose. Carly and her friends wanted to watch the new movie based on a comic book character—*Amazing Girl*. Everyone was talking about it! She walked to the "New Releases" section and quickly scanned the shelves for the title. When she asked the man at the desk, he handed her a copy from a shelf underneath.

"I think that you will really get a kick out of this!" he said with a sly grin.

As Carly took hold of the DVD, a shimmering rainbow light surrounded her. A strong wind lifted her hair and rushed around her body. A buzzing noise filled her ears. Her heart beat rapidly in her chest, but she was too scared to even scream.

The light, noise, and wind all stopped as quickly as they had begun. Carly found herself in a darkened city landscape, wearing a tight pink and green suit with a green cape flowing down her back. Her eyes were shielded by a bright pink mask.

She spun around quickly as she heard a noise behind her. Two masked figures, wearing black clothing were running toward her, each carrying a bag labeled "Sparkles Jewelers." Sirens and alarms screeched in the background.

"Get out of the way!" yelled the first robber. "You don't want to mess with us!"

In the blink of an eye, Carly stuck out her foot and brought her hand down sharply on the neck of the first figure. He crumpled to the ground like a marionette who had lost its strings. The second figure stumbled over his companion as he turned his head to see who was following him. The police reached the men as they scrambled to their feet and prepared to flee.

"Great job again, Amazing Girl!" said the police officer. "It's lucky that you were in the right place at the right time!" He briskly shook Carly by the hand as his men shoved the robbers into a nearby police van.

Carly stared after them in amazement. It had all happened in an instant. How had she managed to stop the robbers? She didn't know how to do karate! And how on Earth was she going to get back to the video store? Was she going to miss her own birthday party . . . ?

A DVD DIMENSION

Right There   Find the answers directly in the text.

Read each sentence. Decide if each statement is **True** or **False**.

1. Carly was picking out some DVDs for her sleepover.   ☐ True   ☐ False

2. Carly was celebrating her seventh birthday.   ☐ True   ☐ False

3. *Amazing Girl* is a movie based on a comic book character.   ☐ True   ☐ False

4. Carly became Amazing Girl and caught the robbers.   ☐ True   ☐ False

Think and Search   Think about what the text says.

Complete the following sentences.

1. Carly and her friends wanted to watch the *Amazing Girl* movie because

_____

_____

_____.

2. The DVD that Carly touched was _____

_____.

3. The two masked men had just _____

_____

_____.

4. When Carly transformed into Amazing Girl, she also gained the ability to ____

_____

_____.

A DVD DIMENSION

On Your Own   Use what you know about the text and your own experience.

1. Write about a comic book character you would like to be. Explain what this character would be able to do.

_____

_____

_____

_____

_____

_____

_____

2. Draw a picture of your comic book character.

A DVD DIMENSION

Predicting

After reading the text on page 15, make a prediction of how the story should end.

1. With a partner, discuss how the story should end. List some ideas to show how Carly could get back to the video store in time for her birthday party.

- _____

   _____

- _____

   _____

   _____

- _____

   _____

2. Complete the table to compare Carly and yourself.

Comparing

Similarities	Differences

Genre: Fable

READING FOCUS

- Analyzes and extracts information from a fable to answer literal, inferential, and applied questions
- Scans text to determine the order of events
- Makes connections between text and his/her own experience to alter events in a text

ANSWER KEY

Right There (Page 21)

1. The ant took a drink because it was a hot day, and he was thirsty.
2. The little ant fell in the river because his feet slipped on a wet rock.
3. a. 4   b. 2   c. 6   d. 1   e. 5   f. 3

Think and Search (Page 21)

1. perched—settled or resting on something
2. thirsty—needing a drink
3. yelled—cried out loudly
4. drown—to die from being underwater too long and inhaling water into the lungs

On Your Own (Page 22)

1. Answers will vary. Possible answer(s): If you are good to others, they will be good to you; one good turn deserves another.
2. Answers will vary. Possible answer(s): kind, friendly, helpful.
3. Answers will vary.

Applying Strategies (Page 23)

1. The ant used the leaf that the dove dropped into the water as a boat.
2. Answers will vary. Possible answer(s): The dove could have used a branch or a vine and pulled the ant out; the dove could have swooped down and gently carried the ant to safety.
3. Answers and drawings will vary.

EXTENSIONS

- "The Ant and the Dove" is one of many of Aesop's fables. Other titles suitable for this age group include the following:
  - "The Dog and the Shadow"
  - "The Fox and the Grapes"
  - "The Tortoise and the Hare"
  - "The Wind and the Sun"
  - "The Lion and the Mouse"
  - "The Town Mouse and the Country Mouse"

Name _____

Read the fable and answer the questions on the following pages.

One hot day, a little ant was crawling along a riverbank.

"How nice and cool the water looks," the ant thought to himself. "I think I'll take a drink." The thirsty ant crawled down to the edge of the river. As he began to drink, his feet slipped on a wet rock, and he fell into the river. The water current began to sweep him away.

"Oh, somebody please help me," the little ant cried out, "or I will surely drown!"

A dove, who was perched on a branch overhanging the river, saw that the ant was in danger.

"I can help him," she thought. "If I drop a leaf into the water, the ant can climb onto it. It will be like a little boat."

So the dove dropped the leaf close to the ant and called out what to do. The ant climbed onto the leaf and soon floated safely to the shore.

"Thank you, kind dove," said the little ant. "You have saved my life. I hope I can help you one day."

A few days later, a hunter came by looking for birds to catch. He saw the dove resting on a branch and began to get out his net. However, the little ant had seen what the hunter was up to. He raced up to the hunter and bit him on the leg. The hunter yelled in pain. The dove heard the noise and flew away to safety. The hunter picked up his net and walked on.

"Thank you this time, little ant," cooed the dove. "You did help me after all."

THE ANT AND THE DOVE

Right There   Find the answers directly in the text.

1. Why did the ant take a drink?

_____

_____

2. Why did the little ant fall in the river?

_____

_____

3. Write the numbers 1 to 6 next to each sentence to show the order of each event in the fable.

a. _____ A hunter got out a net to catch the dove.

b. _____ The dove noticed the ant was in danger.

c. _____ The dove flew away to safety.

d. _____ The ant fell in the river.

e. _____ The ant bit the hunter on the leg.

f. _____ The dove dropped a leaf into the water.

Think and Search   Think about what the text says.

Match each word to its meaning.

1. perched

2. thirsty

3. yelled

4. drown

• cried out loudly

• settled or rested on something

• to die from being underwater too long and inhaling water into the lungs

• needing a drink

THE ANT AND THE DOVE

On Your Own   Use what you know about the text and your own experience.

1. The story of the ant and the dove is a fable. A fable is a story with a moral, which means it teaches us a lesson. What do you think the moral of this story is?

   _____

   _____

   _____

2. List three adjectives that would describe both the ant and the dove.

   • _____

   • _____

   • _____

3. Write about a time you had done a good deed, and in turn, that person did something good.

   _____

   _____

   _____

   _____

   _____

   _____

   _____

   _____

THE ANT AND THE DOVE

Making Connections

After reading the text on page 20, complete the following activity by making the connection between what you already know and the new information from the text.

1. Explain how the dove helped the ant from possibly being drowned.

_____

_____

2. List two other ways the dove could have helped the ant.

- _____

- _____

3. Choose one of your answers from question #2 to change part of the fable of "The Ant and the Dove." Use your own words to fill in the missing lines. Draw a picture in the space below to illustrate how the dove helped the ant in your story.

"Oh, somebody please help me," the little ant cried out, "or I will surely drown!" A dove, who was perched on a branch overhanging the river, saw that the ant was in danger.

"I can help him," she thought. "If I

_____

_____

_____.

So the dove _____

_____

_____.

Genre: Legend

READING FOCUS

- Analyzes and extracts information from a legend to answer literal, inferential, and applied questions
- Makes connections based on prior knowledge, research, and the text
- Synthesizes information to add specified features to an illustration

ANSWER KEY

Right There (Page 26)

1. a. False b. False c. True d. False e. True

2. They told each other stories about their great deeds before they ate.

Think and Search (Page 26)

1. Their meeting place was a round table.

2. He didn't want to favor any particular knight by having one seated at the head of the table.

3. Drawings should depict Arthur pulling "Caliburn" out of a rock.

On Your Own (Page 27)

1. Only the strongest and best knights came to serve King Arthur, so they wanted to be part of this elite group.

2. Answers will vary. Possible answer(s): The Holy Grail was a legend that had been built-up over time; it was a challenge fit for the Knights of the Round Table.

3–4. Answers will vary.

Applying Strategies (Page 28)

Check drawings for accuracy and that all parts are labeled correctly.

EXTENSIONS

- The class can read and discuss stories about the adventures of King Arthur and his knights.
- The class can discuss the character and deeds of Sir Lancelot.
- Students can research and create a list of characters from the Arthurian legends.

(handwritten note on overlapping page: "2 copies pg 20 – 24")

4

Name _____

...nd and answer the questions on the following pages.

...ve been told about King Arthur and his Knights of the Round Table.

...was born, his father promised Merlin, a man of mystery and magic, ...ing up his first son. His father kept his promise and gave Merlin his ...gave Arthur to Sir Ector, whose wife looked after him very well.

...a young man, his father, the king, died. It was said that only ...'d be able to pull an old sword called "Caliburn" out of the rock ...e person to do this would be its rightful owner. Many strong ...they couldn't remove the sword. With Merlin's help, Arthur ...and became king.

...nd best knights came to serve King Arthur. They became ...t deeds and courage.

...sat at a round table so they wouldn't be jealous of the knight chosen to sit at the head of the table. No one at the table could eat until each knight had told a story about something brave or good that he had done. The knights all tried to be the best.

One quest that all the knights were eager to follow was the search for the Holy Grail —a cup that Christian believers consider to be the one that Christ used at the Last Supper.

During one of the many battles Arthur fought, his sword was broken. Merlin took him to the Lady of the Lake, who gave him a very special sword called "Excalibur."

No one knows if the stories about King Arthur are true or even if there really was a King Arthur, but the stories about him and his knights have inspired people for hundreds of years.

KING ARTHUR

Right There   Find the answers directly in the text.

1. Read each sentence. Decide if each statement is **True** or **False**.

   a. Sir Ector was Arthur's real father.   ☐ True   ☐ False

   b. "Excalibur" was stuck in a rock.   ☐ True   ☐ False

   c. Merlin helped Arthur.   ☐ True   ☐ False

   d. Merlin gave Arthur a sword.   ☐ True   ☐ False

   e. Arthur broke "Caliburn."   ☐ True   ☐ False

2. What did the knights do at the Round Table to encourage each other to be good and brave?

   _____

   _____

Think and Search   Think about what the text says.

1. Why were Arthur's knights called "the Knights of the Round Table"?

   _____

   _____

2. Why did King Arthur want them to sit at a round table?

   _____

   _____

   _____

   _____

   _____

   _____

3. Draw what Arthur had to do to become king.

KING ARTHUR

On Your Own   Use what you know about the text and your own experience.

1. Why do you think many young men wanted to
join King Arthur?

_____

_____

_____

2. Why do you think the knights wanted to find the Holy Grail?

_____

_____

_____

3. The stories about King Arthur and his knights have inspired people for hundreds
of years. Why do you think people are inspired by the stories?

_____

_____

_____

4. If you lived in King Arthur's time, would you have liked to have been one of
his knights? Why or why not?

_____

_____

_____

KING ARTHUR

Draw and label each piece of equipment used by knights to fight or to protect themselves in battle.

sword, shield, helmet, gauntlets, lance, shoulder guards, breastplate, thigh guards, boots, spurs

Genre: Fractured Fairy Tale

READING FOCUS

- Analyzes and extracts information from a fractured fairy tale to answer literal, inferential, and applied questions
- Compares a fractured fairy tale with the traditional version
- Determines important information from a text to answer questions

---

ANSWER KEY

Right There (Page 31)

1. . . . people were scared of him; he sometimes lost friends because he accidentally stepped on them.

2. . . . his singing harp and the hen that laid golden eggs.

3. . . . work in the bean field.

Think and Search (Page 31)

Answers and drawings will vary. Possible answer(s):

Gavin—friendly, gentle, nice, giant

Jack—naughty

Jack's mother—friendly, stern

On Your Own (Page 32)

Answers and drawings will vary.

Applying Strategies (Page 33)

1. Answers will vary. Possible answer(s):

   Similarities—both stories had a giant, a beanstalk, a mother with a son named Jack, a golden harp, and a hen that laid golden eggs. Both Jacks stole from the giant.

   Differences—Gavin the Giant was friendly, and the other giant was not so friendly; Gavin befriended Jack, and the other giant wanted to eat Jack; Gavin lived alone, and the other giant lived with his wife; the mother became friends with Gavin, and the other giant did not meet Jack's mother.

2. a. Gavin discovered that Jack had stolen his singing harp and the hen.

   b. Jack's mother stated, "It looks like I have another one of your messes to clean up!"

   c. She climbed the beanstalk with the harp and the hen tied up in her apron.

EXTENSIONS

- Other fractured fairy tales that students may enjoy reading or listening to include the following:
  - *Prince Cinders* by Babette Cole
  - *Princess Prunella and the Purple Peanut* by Margaret Atwood
  - *The Frog Prince Continued* by Jon Scieszka

GAVIN THE GENTLE GIANT

Name _____

Read the fractured fairy tale and answer the questions on the following pages.

Once upon a time, in a land in the clouds, lived a giant named Gavin. He grew his crops of beans and sold them for gold coins. He used some of his gold to buy a harp that sang and a hen that laid golden eggs.

Unfortunately, Gavin didn't have many friends. People were often too scared to come close to him. If they did get to know him, it was often difficult for Gavin to keep friends, as he occasionally stepped on them by mistake. Gavin was a gentle, but lonely, giant!

One day, a boy appeared at the top of the beanstalk. At first, he was too scared to come near Gavin, but Gavin showed him his singing harp and the hen that laid the golden eggs. The boy, Jack, soon became a frequent visitor to Gavin's house.

"At last," Gavin thought, "I have a best friend of my own!"

Gavin even made a special set of bells for Jack to wear whenever he came to visit— just in case Gavin didn't know where he was and accidentally stepped on him!

One cold day when Jack came to visit, Gavin was making hot cocoa. As quick as a wink, Jack snatched the singing harp and the hen and scrambled down the beanstalk. When Gavin discovered his friend and his treasures were gone, he wept huge tears, which flowed out of the clouds and down the beanstalk. Jack was swept from the beanstalk and the treasures were washed from his hands. Jack's mother caught them as they fell to the ground.

"There you are, you naughty child!" she cried. "Now I know what you have been up to— taking what isn't yours! It looks like I have another one of your messes to clean up!"

Jack's mother locked him in his room to recite his multiplication tables. She then climbed the beanstalk with the harp and the hen tied up firmly in her apron.

When she reached the top of the beanstalk, she saw Gavin sleeping quietly on the lawn, exhausted by his tears. He awoke as she came near, and she held out the harp and the hen as a sign of friendship.

"I'm sorry for what my son has done!" she said. "I'll make sure that he is punished."

Jack became a frequent visitor to Gavin's house again. He worked hard every day in the bean field while his mother and Gavin lived happily ever after, drinking cocoa and talking as good friends do!

GAVIN THE GENTLE GIANT

Right There   Find the answers directly in the text.

Complete the following sentences.

1. Gavin didn't have many friends because _____

_____

_____.

2. While Gavin was making cocoa, Jack stole _____

_____

_____.

3. Jack was punished by having to _____

_____

_____.

Think and Search   Think about what the text says.

Write words to describe each character. At the bottom of each box, draw the face of each character.

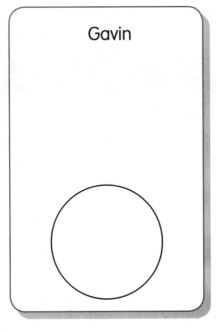

Gavin

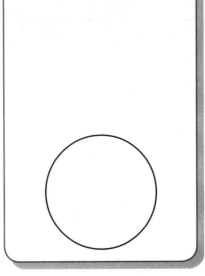

Jack

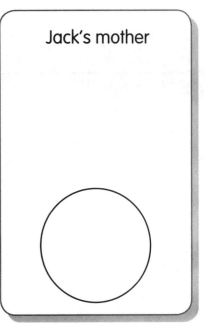

Jack's mother

GAVIN THE GENTLE GIANT

On Your Own   Use what you know about the text and your own experience.

People sometimes say and do not-so-nice things to one another. Think about a not-so-nice interaction you had with someone. Draw a picture and write about the incident. Describe how you felt when it happened.

_____

_____

_____

_____

_____

_____

_____

GAVIN THE GENTLE GIANT

After reading the fractured fairy tale on page 30, make comparisons between "Gavin the Gentle Giant" and "Jack and the Beanstalk."

1. Complete the table by noting similarities and differences between this fractured fairy tale and "Jack and the Beanstalk."

Similarities	Differences

2. Write a sentence using information from the fairy tale to answer the following questions.

a. What incident showed Gavin that Jack was not his friend?

_____

_____

b. How do you know that Jack got into trouble a lot?

_____

_____

c. What things tell you that Jack's mother is a very capable person?

_____

_____

Genre: Biography

READING FOCUS

- Analyzes and extracts information from a biography to answer literal, inferential, and applied questions
- Compares information in a text to his/her own experience
- Makes connections between author and himself/herself

ANSWER KEY

Right There (Page 36)

1. Hill Top Farm in the Lake District of England

2. exploring the fields and woods, catching and taming wild animals, sketching and painting all they saw

3. a. Benjamin Bunny   b. Squirrel Nutkin   c. Tom Kitten

     d. Mr. Brock the badger   e. Jemima Puddleduck   f. Pigling Bland

Think and Search (Page 36)

Answers will vary. Possible answer(s): They enjoyed their summer vacations in the Lake District because they were allowed to just be kids and be carefree; they enjoyed the peace and quiet, which was different than the hustle and bustle of the busy city.

On Your Own (Page 37)

1. Answers will vary. Possible answer(s): accidents around the house, pets chewing things up, pets fighting with one another, pets on the loose.

2. Drawings should show the following animals: hedgehog, dormouse, pig

Applying Strategies (Page 38)

1. a. Beatrix Potter—London; Lake District of England; exploring fields and woods, catching and taming wild animals, and sketching and painting; hedgehog, dormouse, and a pig; be an author of children's stories

     b. You—Answers will vary.

2. Answers will vary.

EXTENSIONS

- Students can draw illustrated story maps of Beatrix Potter stories.
- Students can choose a character from a Beatrix Potter story to describe in full and compare that character with his/her own made-up character.
- Some Beatrix Potter stories include the following:
  - *The Tale of Peter Rabbit*
  - *The Tale of Johnny Town Mouse*
  - *The Tale of Timmy Tiptoes*
  - *The Tale of Two Bad Mice*

Name _____

Read the biography and answer the questions on the following pages.

Children all over the world have grown up enjoying the stories of Peter Rabbit and all the other animals who live at Hill Top Farm in the Lake District of rural England. The creator of these stories was Beatrix Potter, who was born in London in 1866.

As a child, Beatrix and her younger brother, Bertram, spent their summer vacations in the peace and quiet of the Lake District of England, many miles from the hustle and bustle of the busy city. Here, they both discovered a love of nature. The two children spent their days exploring the fields and woods, catching and taming wild animals. They made many sketches and paintings of all they saw.

At home in London, Beatrix and Bertram had many unusual pets, including a hedgehog, a dormouse, and even a pig, which Beatrix bottle-fed. It followed her everywhere, sleeping at night in a basket beside her bed.

Beatrix wrote her first story, *The Tale of Peter Rabbit*, to cheer up a small boy named Noel, who was ill in bed. After some years, the story was published, and it became one of the most famous stories ever written.

Other animal characters include Benjamin Bunny, Tom Kitten, Jemima Puddleduck, Mrs. Tiggywinkle, Squirrel Nutkin, Pigling Bland, Mr. Brock the badger, and Mr. Todd the fox.

When Beatrix Potter married, she bought Hill Top Farm and dedicated her life to preserving the natural beauty of the Lake District. When she died in 1943, she left much of her land to the National Trust, an organization that helps to preserve the beauty of many areas of the country for future generations.

BEATRIX POTTER

Right There   Find the answers directly in the text.

1. Where do the characters of Beatrix Potter's stories live?

_____

_____

2. How did Beatrix and Bertram spend their summer vacations?

_____

_____

3. Complete these characters' names.

  a. Benjamin _____

  b. _____ Nutkin

  c. Tom _____

  d. Mr. _____ the badger

  e. Jemima _____

  f. _____ Bland

Think and Search   Think about what the text says.

Why do you think Beatrix and Bertram enjoyed their summer vacations in the Lake District so much?

_____

_____

_____

_____

_____

BEATRIX POTTER

1. What problems do you think there might have been in the Potters' London home with Beatrix and Bertram's pet collection?

_____

_____

_____

_____

_____

2. Draw pictures of three unusual pets Beatrix and Bertram had.

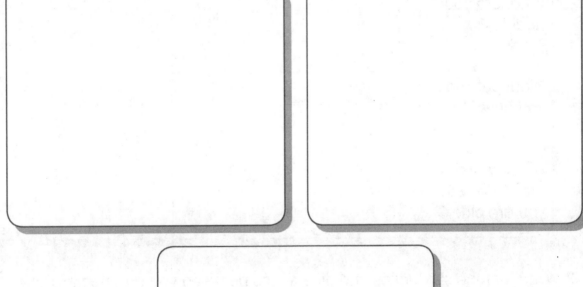

BEATRIX POTTER

Comparing

After reading the text on page 35, make comparisons between you and Beatrix Potter.

1. Imagine you are Beatrix Potter. Answer the question in each box under her name. Then, answer the same questions about yourself.

	Beatrix Potter	You
Where do you live?		
Where do you spend your summer vacations?		
What are your hobbies?		
What pets do you have?		
What would you like to do when you are older?		

2. What are the similarities and differences between you and Beatrix Potter?

Similarities	Differences

Genre: Letter

READING FOCUS

- Analyzes and extracts information from a letter to answer literal, inferential, and applied questions
- Compares formal and informal styles of letter writing
- Synthesizes information from a text to determine its purpose and style

---

ANSWER KEY

Right There (Page 41)

1. a. False   b. True   c. True   d. False   e. True

2. Sarah thinks the farm can be a bit boring at night.

Think and Search (Page 41)

1. He has an appointment with the doctor.

2. They used to be at school together.

3. Sam has moved to a new school in another town.

On Your Own (Page 42)

1. "Snail mail" is sending an actual, physical letter through a postal service as opposed to e-mail.

2. Answers will vary. Possible answer(s):

    Greeting—Dear, Hey there, Hello, To

    Closing—Bye for now, Love, Later, 'Til next time, Ciao, Your friend

Applying Strategies (Page 43)

1. Sarah's—informal; friend; friend; Hi Sam; Catch you later, alligator; Yes; slang and traditional; to stay in touch with a friend.

    Mrs. Robertson's—formal; teacher; parent; Dear Mr. Andrews; Yours sincerely; No; traditional; to communicate with the teacher the situation with the injured toe.

2. Answers will vary. Possible answer(s):

    Formal—letter to a teacher; cover letter for a job you are applying to; letter to a business

    Informal—letter to a friend; letter to a family member

EXTENSIONS

- Students can read examples of formal and informal letters.
- Students can write formal letters for a purpose, such as requesting information from a company or organization.
- Students can write informal letters to pen pals in another school, city, state, or country.

Name _____

Read the letters and answer the questions on the following pages.

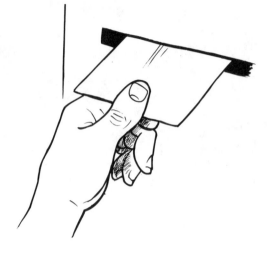

Letter 1

Hi Sam,

Haven't heard from you for ages! What have you been up to?

I can't believe I'm writing a "snail mail"! It's such an old-fashioned thing to do! Why haven't you called me with your new phone number?

Life here is pretty good at the moment. We've got this great new teacher in school. She does lots of fun stuff, not like boring old Mr. Johnson. Do you remember him?

We're off to the farm for vacation again next week. I love it, but it can be a bit b-o-r-i-n-g at night sometimes.

Please, please, please send me a phone number so I can call or text you. I hope all's going well in your new school. What's the town like?

Please get in touch and tell me all your gossip!

Catch you later, alligator,
Sarah

Letter 2

Dear Mr. Andrews,

Please excuse Robert from physical education this week as he has badly bruised the big toe on his left foot. He has been advised by the doctor to rest it for at least one week.

I would also like him to spend recess times sitting quietly, close to the classroom if possible.

Robert has another appointment with the doctor on Friday afternoon. I will pick him up from school at the end of the morning session.

Thank you for your understanding.

Yours sincerely,
Mrs. Robertson (mother)

TWO LETTERS

Right There   Find the answers directly in the text.

1. Read each sentence. Decide if each statment is **True** or **False**.

    a. Mrs. Robertson wrote to Sarah.   ❑ True ❑ False

    b. Sam is at a new school.   ❑ True ❑ False

    c. Sarah is going to the farm for vacation.   ❑ True ❑ False

    d. Mr. Andrews is the doctor.   ❑ True ❑ False

    e. Robert bruised his big toe.   ❑ True ❑ False

2. What does Sarah think about night time on the farm?

_____

_____

Think and Search   Think about what the text says.

1. Why is Robert leaving school early on Friday?

_____

_____

2. How do Sam and Sarah know each other?

_____

_____

3. Why do Sam and Sarah not see each other any more?

_____

_____

TWO LETTERS

On Your Own   Use what you know about the text and your own experience.

1. What do you think Sarah means by a "snail mail"?

_____

_____

2. Sarah's letter to Sam is a friendly, informal letter. What other phrases might be used for the greeting and closing of a friendly letter? List them below.

Greeting

_____

_____

_____

_____

_____

Closing

_____

_____

_____

_____

_____

42   ©Teacher Created Resources

TWO LETTERS

 **Comparing**

After reading the texts on page 40, make a comparison between the two letters.

1. Complete the table to show the differences between the letters.

	Sarah's	Mrs. Robertson's
Type—formal/informal		
Who was it written to? (friend, teacher etc.)		
Who was it written by? (friend, teacher etc.)		
What was the greeting at the start?		
What was the closing at the end?		
Did it have exclamation marks?		
What kind of words were used? (slang, traditional, etc.)		
Why was it written?		

2. Give two reasons to write a formal letter and an informal letter.

Formal	Informal
• _____	• _____
_____	_____
• _____	• _____
_____	_____

Genre: Fantasy

READING FOCUS

- Analyzes and extracts information from a fantasy text to answer literal, inferential, and applied questions
- Uses sensory imaging to describe a place
- Scans a text to find specific words

ANSWER KEY

Right There (Page 46)

1. Green Mist Mountains
2. Darla
3. weary but kind
4. he knew the creatures would accept him

Think and Search (Page 46)

1. They became extinct.
2. All the creatures that lived there were unique.

On Your Own (Page 47)

1. Answers will vary.
2. Drawings will vary.

Applying Strategies (Page 48)

1. Answers will vary. Possible answer(s):

   I can see—trolls, dwarfs, satyrs, witches, goblins, river, trees, secret pathway, clearing, full moon

   I can smell—woods, grass, fresh mountain air

   I can touch—grass, trees, leaves

   I can hear—babbling river, rustling leaves, the various creatures talking

2. Answers will vary.

3. a. said, shouted, echoed, gasped

   b. Five of the following: centaur/troll/dwarf/satyr/witch/goblin

   c. Five of the following: Cirrus/Green Mist Mountains/Darla/Thellon/Sevvy/Bera

EXTENSIONS

- Students may enjoy listening to the following stories:
  - *Pegasus, the Flying Horse* by Jane Yolen*
  - *Half Magic* by Edward Eager
  - *Catwings* by Ursula K. Le Guin

Jane Yolen has written many books about mythical creatures that students may be interested in reading.

Name _____

Read the fantasy story and answer the questions on the following pages.

Cirrus the centaur lived in the Green Mist Mountains with his parents, Thellon and Sevvy, far from humans. The mountains were a magical place inhabited by creatures of all descriptions. The green mist hid the secret places where families of trolls, dwarfs, satyrs, witches, and goblins lived and played.

Cirrus was popular with the other youngsters who lived on the mountain because he was funny and kind. His favorite companion was Darla, the dwarf. Cirrus would gallop through the hills and valleys with Darla clinging to his strong back as they visited their friends. Darla and Cirrus would amuse each other by telling "knock, knock" jokes and limericks.

One day, as Cirrus clambered over some rocks near the riverbed with Darla behind him, they heard moaning from a clump of bushes close by. Darla and Cirrus came to a sudden stop as the bushes rustled and swayed. A creature carefully rose from underneath. It was a very odd-looking creature with the head of a lion, the body of a goat, and the tail of a serpent. Its face was weary but kind.

"Don't be scared!" the creature gasped. "My name is Bera. I have traveled a long way to find the Green Mist Mountains. I am the last of my kind in the world. I only wish to find a peaceful place to spend my remaining days. I have heard that the creatures of the Green Mist Mountains are many and varied so will accept me as I am." Darla and Cirrus led Bera from the river through the secret pathways into the Green Mist Mountains. A sea of unusual creatures greeted them as they reached the main clearing. Bera told his story and was allowed to settle in the forest. He kept to himself and didn't join any of the activities the other grown-ups did.

Cirrus, being the kind centaur that he was, decided to think of a plan to cheer up Bera. When the next full moon arrived, Cirrus coaxed Bera into the main clearing where a huge circle of fire blazed. He urged Bera to sit in a spot at the front among the other creatures. One by one, each creature or group of creatures came to the center of the ring to show their talents. The trolls lifted heavy tree trunks high above their heads. The satyrs sped around the circle until a cloud of mist encircled everyone's heads. The blue witches performed vanishing tricks, and the goblins snuck into the crowd and revealed items they had taken without anyone noticing.

Cirrus was the last to appear. "Knock, knock!"

"Who's there?" said the crowd.

"Bera!" shouted Cirrus.

"Bera who?" echoed the crowd.

"Bera late than never!" said Cirrus.

A tiny smile lifted the corners of Bera's mouth.

CIRRUS THE CENTAUR'S SHOW

Right There   Find the answers directly in the text.

Complete each sentence with words from the story.

1. Cirrus lived with his parents in the _____

_____.

2. The name of Cirrus's best friend was _____.

3. The strange creature's face was _____

_____.

4. Bera wanted to live there because _____

_____

_____.

Think and Search   Think about what the text says.

1. What most likely happened to the other creatures like Bera?

_____

_____

_____

2. Why do you think the creatures in the Green Mist Mountains accepted Bera so easily?

_____

_____

_____

CIRRUS THE CENTAUR'S SHOW

On Your Own   Use what you know about the text and your own experience.

1. Use the space below to write your own "knock, knock" joke to tell to a friend.

_____

_____

_____

_____

_____

_____

_____

_____

_____

2. Draw a picture of a mythical creature that might live in the Green Mist Mountains.

CIRRUS THE CENTAUR'S SHOW

Use the fantasy story on page 45 to complete the following activity by using your senses to create a mental image of what you have read.

1. Use your imagination to write about the Green Mist Mountains.

I can see . . .	I can smell . . .
I can touch . . .	I can hear . . .

2. Write a sentence to describe how you would feel to discover a creature from the Green Mist Mountains.

_____

_____

3. Scan the text to find and write:

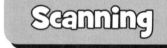

a. four words that mean "different ways of talking."

_____

b. the names of five imaginary creatures.

_____

c. five creature or place names.

_____

Genre: Mystery

READING FOCUS

- Analyzes and extracts information from a mystery narrative to answer literal, inferential, and applied questions
- Uses sensory imaging to create appropriate background information for a mystery narrative text
- Predicts likely events that could take place after the close of a mystery narrative text

ANSWER KEY

Right There (Page 51)

1. He was great at solving mysteries.
2. • small handwriting
   • grubby fingerprints
   • the name "Tom" was rubbed into the paper
3. a. True   b. False   c. False   d. True   e. True

Think and Search (Page 51)

1. Answers will vary. Possible answer(s): all three Toms have dirty hands, Ben doesn't know any of the boys named Tom.
2. Answers will vary. Possible answer(s): good problem-solver, smart, thorough, detail-oriented.

On Your Own (Page 52)

Answers will vary.

Applying Strategies (Page 53)

1. a–d. Answers will vary.
2. Answers will vary.

EXTENSIONS

- Other mystery stories the students might enjoy include the following:
  - *Antonio S and the Mystery of Theodore Guzman* by Odo Hirsch
  - *Emily Eyefinger* series by Duncan Ball
  - *Encyclopedia Brown* series by Donald J. Sobol

Name _____

Read the mystery and answer the questions on the following pages.

"Who do you think left this for you?"

Ben frowned. "I have no idea."

I took the note from him and read it again.

> *Don't you dare tell my secret. If you do, you will be sorry.*
> *I will take your favorite things.*

"I don't know any secrets!" Ben said. "It's crazy. What should I do, Jeremy?"

Ben had come to me because I was great at solving mysteries. So far this term, I had solved the mystery of what had happened to Lucy's lunch money and Miss Spencer's silver pen. But this was more difficult. Ben had found the note on his desk after recess with no sign of who might have left it.

"Let's look at the clues," I said. "The handwriting is small, so it's someone older than us. And there's lots of grubby fingerprints, so it's someone who doesn't keep their hands too clean." I peered at the note more closely. "The person must have placed a paper on top of the note to write something else. There's a name rubbed into it. It says . . . Tom. That's who we're looking for."

"But there are heaps of boys named Tom at this school!" Ben wailed. "How do we know which one it is?"

"I'll make a list of the most likely suspects," I said.

Over the next two days, I discovered there were only three boys named Tom at our school who were older than we were. All of them looked as if they would usually have dirty hands. Ben swore he had never spoken to any of them. I began to wonder if the note had been put on his desk by mistake. But on Friday, a toy that Ben had brought to school for share day disappeared from Miss Spencer's cupboard. In its place was another note.

> *I warned you not to tell anyone, but you didn't listen.*
> *Don't do it again.*

DON'T YOU DARE TELL

Right There   Find the answers directly in the text.

1. Why was Ben asking Jeremy for help?

_____

2. List the three clues Jeremy found on the note.

- _____

- _____

- _____

3. Read each sentence. Decide if each statement is **True** or **False**.

a. The first note was left on Ben's desk. ☐ True ☐ False

b. There was only one boy named Tom at Ben and Jeremy's school. ☐ True ☐ False

c. Ben brought a silver pen to school for share day. ☐ True ☐ False

d. The second note was found in Miss Spencer's cupboard. ☐ True ☐ False

e. Jeremy had found out what had happened to Lucy's lunch money. ☐ True ☐ False

Think and Search   Think about what the text says.

1. Name two things that might make this mystery difficult to solve.

- _____

- _____

2. List words to describe the sort of person you think Jeremy is.

_____

_____

_____

DON'T YOU DARE TELL

Describe how you would feel if you had received Ben's mysterious notes. How would you try to solve the mystery?

_____

_____

_____

_____

_____

_____

_____

_____

_____

_____

_____

_____

_____

DON'T YOU DARE TELL

Predicting   After reading the text on page 50, predict what may have happened before and what might happen next.

1. Think about what might have taken place before the story began by answering the questions below. You can be as creative as you like!

   a. Who do you think is leaving the notes for Ben?

   _____

   _____

   b. What secret does he/she think Ben has found out?

   _____

   _____

   c. Why does he/she think it is Ben who is telling the secret?

   _____

   _____

   d. Who is really telling the secret?

   _____

   _____

2. Consider your answers from question #1 and the story on page 50 to help you predict what will happen next in the story. What steps do you think Jeremy will take to find the culprit? Will he succeed?

   _____

   _____

   _____

   _____

   _____

Genre: Suspense

READING FOCUS

- Analyzes and extracts information from a suspense narrative to answer literal, inferential, and applied questions
- Uses sensory imaging to create emotional and visual images based on personal background knowledge and experiences
- Predicts and explains events using the text and background information
- Summarizes text by identifying keywords

ANSWER KEY

Right There (Page 56)

1. boring
2. weird music; screaming her head off
3. she could get her hands on
4. bad idea
5. still there; nowhere to be seen

Think and Search (Page 56)

1. a. No   b. Yes   c. Yes   d. Yes   e. No
2. "Sobbing, Bev pulled and pulled"; "yelling frantically"; "Bev screamed in horror"

On Your Own (Page 57)

1. Answers will vary.
2. Bev was scared and worried because she couldn't pull Jan out of the mud.
3. Answers will vary. Possible answer(s): No, they just have sibling rivalry.

Applying Strategies (Page 58)

1. a. Answers will vary. Possible answer(s): scared, panicked, worried, frightened, frantic.
   b. Drawing should depict Jan looking scared.
2. a–b. Answers will vary.
3. a–b. Summary should include:
   - The family went for a drive in the country.
   - The girls were fighting.
   - They stopped for a picnic lunch.
   - Bev and Jan decided to go for a walk.
   - Jan thought cutting across the marsh would be fun.
   - Jan got stuck in the mud.
   - Bev ran back to get help from Mom and Dad.
   - Jan was nowhere to be seen.

EXTENSIONS

- Students can write a summary of the story based on the keywords selected.
- Students can create a collage by cutting out faces from magazines and placing them in categories according to the feeling (emotion) students believe is reflected on each face.
- Students can write a character profile of a friend or family member. For example, physical characteristics, personality, activities, and likes and dislikes.

Name _____

Read the suspense story and answer the questions on the following pages.

After days of miserable wet weather, seeing the blue sky was wonderful. Dad decided the family should go for a drive into the country.

"Do we have to?" moaned Jan. "It's so boring just driving and driving to nowhere and back again. I hate it."

"Don't you complain. I have to put up with Dad's weird music and Susie screaming her head off while you sit with headphones on, doing nothing. You're selfish and mean and I hate you," her sister Bev added.

"Girls, girls, can't you stop fighting just for a change?" Mom begged. "We'll take a picnic lunch; you might even enjoy it."

It seemed to take forever, until Dad finally stopped the car. They all got out, unpacked the food, and had lunch.

Susie ate everything she could get her hands on and fell asleep. Mom and Dad were comfortable in their chairs and obviously wouldn't be going home for a while. The two older girls decided to go for a walk. After trudging along the trail for a while, Jan thought it would be fun to surprise Mom and Dad by coming back to the picnic spot from the opposite direction. They would have to cut across the marsh back to the main road.

Bev thought it was a bad idea, like most things her sister did, but she couldn't be bothered with arguing. She followed Jan across the marsh.

"Yuck! It's horrible. Don't come this way! I'm sinking," Jan complained.

Bev stopped and looked at her sister, who was up past her knees in the mud. "I'm stuck, really stuck. I can't get out!"

As Bev watched, Jan seemed to be slipping down further into the sticky mud. She found a thin branch and told Jan to grab it. Sobbing, Bev pulled and pulled, but Jan didn't move. She didn't want to leave, but she knew she had to get help fast.

Mom and Dad heard her yelling frantically as she came running up the trail. They rushed to meet her and followed her back. When they got there, Bev screamed in horror. The branch was still there, but her sister was nowhere to be seen.

THE MARSHES

| **Right There** | Find the answers directly in the text. |

Complete the following sentences with words from the story.

1. Jan thought that it was _____ just driving and driving to nowhere and back.

2. Bev had to put up with Dad's _____ and

   Susie _____.

3. Susie ate everything _____ and fell asleep.

4. Bev thought that it was a _____ to cut across the marsh.

5. The branch was _____, but Jan was

   _____.

| **Think and Search** | Think about what the text says. |

1. Read each sentence. Choose **Yes** or **No**.

   a. The girls went for a walk in the rain.   ☐ Yes   ☐ No

   b. Susie was Bev's younger sister.   ☐ Yes   ☐ No

   c. Jan couldn't hear her father's music.   ☐ Yes   ☐ No

   d. Their parents were enjoying the picnic.   ☐ Yes   ☐ No

   e. The girls got along well together.   ☐ Yes   ☐ No

2. List words and phrases from the text that show Bev was upset about the situation.

   • _____

   • _____

   • _____

THE MARSHES

On Your Own   Use what you know about the text and your own experience.

1. Which sister do you think is the oldest? Why?

_____

_____

_____

_____

2. Why was Bev sobbing as she tried to pull Jan out of the mud?

_____

_____

_____

_____

3. Do you think Bev really disliked Jan? Explain why you think this.

_____

_____

_____

_____

THE MARSHES

Sensory Imaging

After reading the text on page 55, complete the following activities by using your senses to create a mental image of what you have read.

1. a. How do you think Jan was feeling when she realized she was stuck? Write words to describe her feelings.

_____

_____

_____

_____

_____

b. Draw Jan in the mud. Try to make your drawing show how she feels.

2. The story doesn't tell you what happened to Jan.

Predicting

a. What do you think happened? _____

_____

_____

b. Write a happy ending to the story. _____

_____

_____

3. a. Read "The Marshes" again. Underline the key phrases in the story. They should provide you with the main points for making a summary, which is a shorter form of the original story.

Summarizing

b. Compare the key phrases you underlined with a partner's key phrases, and decide if you need to add more words or take out any words that you don't need.

Genre: Movie Review

READING FOCUS

- Analyzes and extracts information from a movie review to answer literal, inferential, and applied questions
- Uses sensory imaging to describe a character's experiences in a scene
- Scans text to locate specific information
- Predicts the ending of an adventure story

ANSWER KEY

Right There (Page 61)

1. Cale Cooper
2. 12 years old
3. Blair Hunter
4. Simon Bergman
5. Jenny Jackson

Think and Search (Page 61)

1. The DVD remote control has a part in controlling what happens in the movie.

2. Answers could include: new hit, action-packed, nail-biting adventures, children get a thrill watching.

On Your Own (Page 62)

1. a–b. Answers will vary.

2–3. Answers will vary.

Applying Strategies (Page 63)

1. Answers will vary. Possible answer(s):

   What Blair saw—staircase, castle, lightning, furniture covered in dustsheets, ghostly figure

   What Blair heard—creaky staircase, thunder, wind howling

   Blair's feelings—scared, nervous, anxious

2. Answers will vary.

EXTENSIONS

- Students can write a review and give a rating of up to five stars for a movie they have watched.
- Teacher can share newspapers that include movie reviews, which can be read as a whole class and discussed.

Name _____

Read the movie review and answer the questions on the following pages.

Popular movie director, Simon Bergman, has once again produced a blockbuster with his new hit, *Remote Control*, starring 12-year-old Cale Cooper.

In the movie, Cale plays the part of Blair Hunter, who receives a DVD player for his birthday from his computer whiz relative, Uncle Lindsay. His uncle also includes a DVD for Blair to watch. As he settles down in a comfy chair and begins to watch the DVD, to his surprise he realizes that the main character in the movie is actually Blair himself! He looks the same, sounds the same, and even has the same name!

Blair finds that he is watching himself becoming involved in a series of adventures. In one scene, Blair is walking up a creaky staircase in what seems to be a castle. The wind is howling outside and sneaks into the building through cracks and under doorways. Claps of thunder drown out the sound of the wind and lightning brightens up the dark house. Blair can make out furniture covered in dustsheets. Suddenly, at the top of the stairs, he sees a ghostly figure. Both "Blairs" scream in fright. The Blair in the chair presses "Stop" on the DVD remote control. When he has the courage to press "Play" again, he finds himself in a different adventure!

The movie continues with Blair discovering he can press the stop button to end the adventure and the play button to start another one. However, this changes when he decides to press "Rewind." Instead of the adventure changing, it goes back to where it ended. And this time "Stop" will not work! No matter how scared he becomes, he is forced to watch.

Remote Control will have movie theaters packed during the summer as children get a thrill watching Blair's experiences. While the movie is action-packed and involves many nail-biting adventures, it is still rated G.

My rating:
★★★★☆

REMOTE CONTROL

Right There Find the answers directly in the text.

Write a short answer for the following questions.

1. Who starred in the movie? _____

2. How old is he? _____

3. What character did he play? _____

4. Who directed the movie? _____

5. Who wrote the review? _____

Think and Search Think about what the text says.

1. Why is the movie called *Remote Control*?

_____

_____

2. The movie was given a score of four stars by the reviewer. Add words and phrases in the box below that the reviewer used that showed her opinion about the movie. Two are given for you.

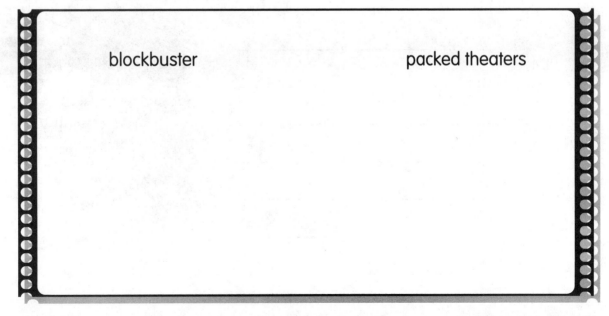

blockbuster   packed theaters

REMOTE CONTROL

On Your Own Use what you know about the text and your own experience.

1. **a.** After reading the review, do you agree
   that the rating should be G? ☐ Yes ☐ No

   b. Give a reason for your answer.

   _____

   _____

   _____

   _____

   _____

   _____

2. Think of another title for this movie.

   _____

   _____

   _____

3. Would *Remote Control* be a movie you
   would like to see? Explain why or why not.

   _____

   _____

   _____

   _____

   _____

   _____

   _____

REMOTE CONTROL

After reading the text on page 60, complete the following activity by using your senses to create a mental image of what you have read.

1. Read paragraph 3 of the review. Use words and phrases from the text and your own imagination to describe Blair's experiences in the castle.

What Blair saw	What Blair heard
Blair's feelings	

2. Imagine Blair decided to press "Rewind" instead of "Stop" when he saw the ghostly figure in the castle and the adventure begins again from that moment. Describe what you think will happen next in the movie and how the adventure might end.

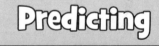

_____

_____

_____

_____

_____

_____

Genre: Play

READING FOCUS

- Analyzes and extracts information from a play to answer literal, inferential, and applied questions
- Makes connections between the features of a playscript and his/her own ideas to plan a new playscript with the same characters
- Determines the importance of information in a playscript to plan his/her own playscript with the same characters

ANSWER KEY

Right There (Page 66)

1. She had moved perfectly, remembered all her lines, and sung in tune.

2. Ethan tripped on the stage and couldn't stop laughing; Amy forgot her lines and said silly things; and David's guitar string broke, making his song sound weird.

Think and Search (Page 66)

1. Answers will vary. Possible answer(s): confident, overachiever.

2. drama teacher

On Your Own (Page 67)

1–3. Answers will vary.

Applying Strategies (Page 68)

1–2. Answers will vary.

EXTENSIONS

- Students can present plays adapted from popular children's books. Some suggested titles include:
  - *Charlie and the Chocolate Factory* by Roald Dahl
  - *The Lion, the Witch and the Wardrobe* by C.S. Lewis
  - *Charlotte's Web* by E.B. White

THE SCHOOL PLAY

Name _____

Read the play and answer the questions on the following pages.

Three children in school uniform, Amy, David, and Ethan, are sitting outside a door. On the door is a sign that reads "SCHOOL PLAY AUDITIONS TODAY."

Amy   How much longer do you think Mr. Dodd will be?

David   He said there was just Olivia left to audition. Then he said he'd tell the people waiting outside if they got a part in the play or not.

Ethan   I don't even know why I'm waiting. My audition was terrible. I tripped on the stage. I couldn't stop laughing.

Amy   That doesn't sound any worse than my audition. I forgot my lines, so I had to make them up. I said the silliest things!

David   You don't have anything to worry about. I decided to play my guitar and sing for my audition. But one of my strings broke, and I had to play and sing without it! The song sounded really weird.

Ethan   It sounds like none of us have any hope of being in the play.

Amy   Maybe we should just go.

All three nod and stand up. Suddenly, the door opens, and Olivia walks out.

David   How do you think you did, Olivia?

Olivia   *(tossing her head and smiling)* I was great! I moved perfectly, I remembered all my lines, and I sang in tune. I'm sure to get a main role.

The door opens again. Mr. Dodd steps out.

Mr. Dodd   Is it just you four waiting to find out who got a part in the play?

They all nod.

Mr. Dodd   Well, I'm happy to tell you that you were all successful. Congratulations!

Olivia   Is mine the main role?

Mr. Dodd   No, I'm sorry, Olivia. I had to give the main roles to Amy, David, and Ethan.

Ethan   What? Why would you give us the main roles? We all did terrible auditions. We were clumsy, we forgot our lines, and we sang badly.

Mr. Dodd   Yes, I know. You were perfect for this year's play. It's set at a circus . . . and the main characters are clowns!

Mr. Dodd smiles. Amy, David, and Ethan begin to laugh. Olivia stomps her foot and exits.

THE SCHOOL PLAY

Right There   Find the answers directly in the text.

1. Why did Olivia think she might have been given the main role in the play?

_____

_____

2. List three things that went wrong in the main characters' auditions.

- _____

_____

- _____

_____

- _____

_____

Think and Search   Think about what the text says.

1. What sort of person do you think Olivia is? What makes you think this?

_____

_____

2. Place an **X** in the box next to the job Mr. Dodd is most likely to have.

❏ school principal

❏ gardener

❏ drama teacher

❏ math teacher

THE SCHOOL PLAY

Use what you know about the text and your own experience.

1. If you were Mr. Dodd, would you have given the main roles to Amy, David, and Ethan? Explain why/why not.

   _____

   _____

   _____

   _____

2. The next time Olivia auditions for a play, do you think she will behave differently? Give a reason for your answer.

   _____

   _____

   _____

   _____

3. Imagine you were auditioning for a school play. Write some words to describe some of the feelings you may have. For example, would you be nervous or cool as a cucumber?

   _____

   _____

   _____

   _____

THE SCHOOL PLAY

Determining Importance

Use the text on page 65 to help you determine the important parts of a playscript.

1. Imagine the auditions of Amy, David, and Ethan. Plan a short playscript that describes what happened.

Beginning of Playscript

- Playscripts often begin with a brief description of the setting.

  Describe the audition room and who is in it when your play begins.

  _____

  _____

  _____

- Who says the first line in your play? What does he/she say?

  _____

  _____

  _____

Middle of Playscript

- Choose an audition piece for each character. It should be something you know well (e.g., a nursery rhyme, a favorite song).

  Amy _____

  David _____

  Ethan _____

- Describe some of Mr. Dodd's reactions to the auditions.

  _____

  _____

  _____

End of Playscript

- Who says the final line in the play? What does he/she say?

  _____

  _____

- Playscripts often end with a description of the characters' reactions to the final line. Describe what the characters do at the end of your play.

  _____

  _____

---

2. Use the plan above to help you write your playscript on a separate sheet of paper.

Genre: Informational Text —Flow Chart

READING FOCUS

- Analyzes and extracts information from a flow chart to answer literal, inferential, and applied questions
- Scans visual and written text to determine importance of information
- Summarizes information by recording keywords and phrases from a flow chart

ANSWER KEY

Right There (Page 71)

1. A cow is able to make milk after it has had a calf.

2. hay, clover, water, grass, grains

3. a. Milk is stored in the cow's <u>udder</u>.

   b. A cow needs milking <u>twice</u> a day.

   c. <u>Before</u> a cow is milked, the farmer washes the cow's <u>udder</u>.

Think and Search (Page 71)

1. a. so that the milk will be safe to drink

   b. so that the milk is drinkable without any solid parts

2.

On Your Own (Page 72)

Drawings will vary.

Applying Strategies (Page 73)

1. A cow needs to eat plenty of food, such as grass, clover, grains, and hay. It also needs to drink about 40 gallons of water each day.

2. Milk is stored in the cow's udder—a large bag.

3. The udder is washed, and a machine is then hooked up to the cow's udder. The milk is pumped into tanks and kept cool.

4. The milk is pasteurized and homogenized. The milk is either put into containers or used to make other dairy products.

EXTENSIONS

- Students can create their own flow charts, either individually, in pairs, or in small groups, for the following processes:
  - The Story of Bread ("From Wheat to You")
  - The Story of the Recycling of a Particular Item
  - The Story of How a Letter Gets to Its Destination

Name _____

Read the flow chart and answer the questions on the following pages.

A cow makes milk after it has a calf. It can make up to 10 gallons of milk each day.

A cow needs to eat lots of food, such as grass, clover, grains, and hay, to make good quality milk. It also needs to drink about 40 gallons of water each day.

Milk is stored in the cow's udder, which is like a large bag. A cow needs to be milked at least twice a day.

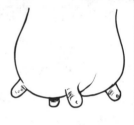

A refrigeration truck comes to pick up the milk daily and takes it to a special processing plant.

Before a cow is milked, the farmer washes the udder. A machine is attached to the udder. The milk is pumped into large tanks and kept cool.

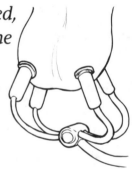

There it is tested and checked to make sure it is fresh and healthy.

The milk is quickly heated to 162°F for 15 seconds to kill any bacteria (germs). This process is called "pasteurization."

The milk is then forced through a sieve (a container with tiny holes) to break up any "lumps" of fat. This process is called "homogenization."

The milk is put into bottles or cartons and taken to the stores for us to buy. It can also be used to make other products, such as butter, cream, ice cream, cheese, and yogurt.

FROM THE COW TO YOU

Right There   Find the answers directly in the text.

1. When is a cow able to make milk?

_____

2. Place an **X** next to the things a cow needs to consume to make good
quality milk.

☐ hay   ☐ meat   ☐ clover   ☐ milk

☐ water   ☐ grass   ☐ bark   ☐ grains

3. The sentences below are incorrect. Rewrite each sentence so it is correct.

a. Milk is stored in the cow's stomach.

_____

b. A cow needs milking once a day.

_____

c. After a cow is milked, the farmer washes the cow's feet.

_____

Think and Search   Think about what the text says.

1. Why are each of the following
processes important?

a. pasteurization

_____

_____

b. homogenization

_____

_____

2. Circle and label the picture of a
sieve you might use in a kitchen.

FROM THE COW TO YOU

On Your Own   Use what you know about the text and your own experience.

Draw and label four milk products you like to use.

FROM THE COW TO YOU

Summarizing

Use the text on page 70 to write brief notes about the story of milk under each heading. Highlight or underline important words and phrases on page 70 before you write your answers.

1. What a cow needs to make milk

2. Description of where a cow stores milk

3. How a cow is milked

4. What happens to the milk at the processing plant

READING FOCUS

- Analyzes and extracts information from a procedure to answer literal, inferential, and applied questions
- Scans a text to find verbs
- Synthesizes the structure of a procedure to create his/her own procedure

ANSWER KEY

Right There (Page 76)

1. a. 4 Add food coloring to the mixture.
   b. 1 Roll up your sleeves.
   c. 6 Scrape around the sides of the bowl.
   d. 10 Wrap the slime in plastic wrap.
   e. 9 Throw the slime onto the board.
2. a. In step 5, you should stir the mixture until it becomes very difficult to stir.
   b. You can add three to six drops of food coloring, depending on how green you would like your slime.

Think and Search (Page 76)

1. It can get very messy.
2. to emphasize that you should add the water one drop at a time

On Your Own (Page 77)

1–2. Answers will vary.

3. Answers will vary. Possible answer(s): slimy, gooey, sticky, thick.

Applying Strategies (Page 78)

1. put, add, use, drop, add, tip, slap, hold, roll, wrap
2. Answers will vary.

EXTENSIONS

- Teachers can integrate literacy with science and use the procedure to make slime. Students can rate the instructions on a scale of 1 (easy to follow) to 5 (difficult/confusing to follow).

Note: *Teachers are advised to try making slime prior to the activity as it will be easier to direct how much water to add.*

HOW TO MAKE SLIME

Name _____

Read the procedure and answer the questions on the following pages.

What You Need:

- 1 cup of cornstarch
- 3 to 6 drops of green food coloring
- eyedropper
- wooden board or cutting board
- water (in a container)
- plastic wrap
- mixing spoon
- mixing bowl
- apron

What You Do:

1 Put on your apron, roll up your sleeves, and tie back your hair (if it is long).

2 Add the cornstarch to the mixing bowl.

3 Use the eyedropper to add drops of water to the cornstarch VERY SLOWLY and mix it with the spoon.

4 Drop between three to six drops of green food coloring into the mixture (depending on how green you would like your slime.)

5 Add more drops of water to the mixture and stir it until it becomes very difficult to stir.

6 Tip the slime out onto the board, scraping around the sides of the bowl.

7 Slap the slime with your hand. It should feel hard like a solid object.

8 Hold the slime in your hand and open your fingers. Let the slime run through your fingers like a liquid. (If it doesn't, put it back in the bowl and add more water—not too much!)

9 Roll the slime into a ball and throw it onto the board. What does it do?

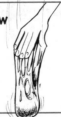

10 Wrap the slime in plastic wrap and take it home. Impress your family with the mystery of your slimy creation!

HOW TO MAKE SLIME

Right There   Find the answers directly in the text.

1. Write the step number that matches the instruction.

   a. _____ Add food coloring to the mixture.

   b. _____ Roll up your sleeves.

   c. _____ Scrape around the sides of the bowl.

   d. _____ Wrap the slime in plastic wrap.

   e. _____ Throw the slime onto the board.

2. Finish these sentences.

   a. In step 5, you should stir the mixture until it . . .

   _____

   _____ .

   b. You can add three to six drops of food coloring, depending on . . .

   _____

   _____ .

Think and Search   Think about what the text says.

1. Why should you wear an apron when making slime?

   _____

   _____

2. Why do you think the words *very slowly* are in capital letters in step 3?

   _____

   _____

HOW TO MAKE SLIME

1. Do you think you could follow this
procedure to make slime?   ☐ Yes   ☐ No

2. Why do you think the writer calls the slimy creation a "mystery"?

_____

_____

_____

_____

_____

_____

_____

_____

_____

3. List four adjectives to describe slime.

- _____

- _____

- _____

- _____

HOW TO MAKE SLIME

Scanning

Scan the text on page 75, and locate specific details to help you complete the following activity.

1. A verb is a "doing" word. Texts that give instructions usually start with a verb. List the verbs that begin the instructions in "How to Make Slime." (Some are the same.)

_____

_____

_____

2. Think of something that you know how to do, such as making breakfast, making your bed, or setting the table. Write a procedure for this, and start each instruction with a verb. Add some pictures.

Synthesizing

How to _____

❶	❷

❸	❹

Unit 15
April Fools!

Genre: Humor

READING FOCUS

- Analyzes and extracts information from a humorous recount to answer literal, inferential, and applied questions
- Scans text to determine the order of events
- Summarizes information by recording keywords and phrases
- Compares own reactions with the characters' reactions to situations in a text

---

ANSWER KEY

Right There (Page 81)

1. four

2. Sophie and Kelly

3. a. Dad—looked puzzled, then laughed

   b. Sophie—screamed, then went off in a huff

   c. Kelly—felt disgusted, then agreed it was a good trick

   d. Mom—giggled and asked why she kept being tickled

Think and Search (Page 81)

1. to laugh so hard, or so long, that your ribs hurt

2. April 1

3. Jamie's mom switched out the sugar for the salt.

On Your Own (Page 82)

Answers will vary.

Applying Strategies (Page 83)

Answers will vary.

EXTENSIONS

- Students can compile a list of safe April Fool's Day jokes to play on friends or family and illustrate each one. They should discuss the appropriateness of each before adding it to the list.

Name _____

Read the humorous recount and answer the questions on the following pages.

Wow, what a day! My stomach is still aching from laughing so much. Now I know what the saying, "Laugh until your sides split," means! Today was a Saturday, and it also happened to be April Fool's Day—April 1. I had decided to play some April Fool's Day jokes on my family.

First, it was Dad's turn. He always reads the newspaper first thing Saturday mornings. I set my alarm for 6:30 a.m. and fetched the paper from the front lawn. After carefully unwrapping it, I swapped all the pages around. Then, I rolled it up in its plastic wrapping again and put it back on the lawn for him to pick up later. You should have seen the puzzled look on his face when he opened it! He turned it upside down and back to front. I popped out from behind the door and said, "Look at the date on the paper, Dad!" He looked and started to laugh as I gleefully called out, "April fools!"

My younger sister was easy to fool. She fell for the "plastic spider trick." As she was about to sit at the table for breakfast I yelled, "Sophie, watch out for that spider!" She screamed and jumped in the air. When I said, "April fools!" she went off in a huff back to her room. Dad and I laughed even harder.

Next, it was my older sister's turn. In one hand I had a black beetle I found in the garden and in the other I had a black jelly bean. I showed Kelly the beetle, then swapped objects when she looked away. I put what she thought was the beetle in my mouth. "You're gross, Jamie!" she said in disgust. But she admitted it was a great trick after I said, "April fools!" and showed her the chewed jelly bean and the beetle in my other hand.

To trick Mom, I stuck a note on her back that said "Tickle me!" After being tickled a few times by each of us she giggled, "Why does everyone feel like tickling me today?" She giggled even more when I exclaimed, "April fools!"

But the jokes hadn't ended yet. Mom made some delicious hot chocolate for breakfast. I added a spoonful of sugar and took a sip. Yuck! I spat it back into the cup.

"April fools!" Mom laughed, as she showed me the salt container and the "sugar" bowl!

APRIL FOOLS!

Right There   Find the answers directly in the text.

1. Place an **X** next to the number of people Jamie tricked on April Fool's Day.

❑ five   ❑ three   ❑ one   ❑ four   ❑ two

2. What were the names of Jamie's sisters? _____

_____

3. Match what each person did when Jamie tricked him or her.

a. Dad   • screamed, then went off in a huff.

b. Sophie   • giggled and asked why she kept being tickled.

c. Kelly   • looked puzzled, then laughed.

d. Mom   • felt disgusted, then agreed it was a good trick.

Think and Search   Think about what the text says.

1. Explain what Jamie meant by the saying, "laugh until your sides split."

_____

_____

2. What date would Dad have seen on the paper?

_____

3. Explain how Jamie was tricked.

_____

_____

_____

_____

APRIL FOOLS!

On Your Own   Use what you know about the text and your own experience.

Describe a day of tricks you would play on members of your family.

_____

_____

_____

_____

_____

_____

_____

_____

_____

_____

_____

_____

_____

_____

_____

_____

_____

APRIL FOOLS!

Use the text on page 80 to complete the activities. Use keywords and phrases to describe each April Fool's Day joke. Make up a name for each (e.g., "The Plastic Spider Trick"), and list them in the order they happened.

Next to each joke, write words to describe how you would have felt if the joke had been played on you (e.g., angry, puzzled, amused, scared).

Joke's Name and Description	My Reaction
Joke 1 _____ _____	
Joke 2 _____ _____	
Joke 3 _____ _____	
Joke 4 _____ _____	
Joke 5 _____ _____	

Genre: Poetry

READING FOCUS

- Analyzes and extracts information from a poem to answer literal, inferential, and applied questions
- Scans a text to identify rhyming words
- Synthesizes the structure of a poem to write another poem with a similar theme

ANSWER KEY

Right There (Page 86)

1. a. two   b. calm   c. Bubble

2. The daughters are missing great big clumps of hair.

3. Jojo rode around on the cat.

Think and Search (Page 86)

1. Jojo came from the pet shop.

2. A parent (poem says "our two daughters")

3. Answers will vary. Possible answer(s):

    a. excited, happy   b. angry, frustrated   c. excited, happy, content, relieved

On Your Own (Page 87)

1. Answers will vary.

2. fair/hair, that/cat, disaster/faster, Bubble/trouble

3. Answers will vary.

Applying Strategies (Page 88)

1–2. Answers will vary.

3. Drawing should depict what each student's poem is about.

EXTENSIONS

- Students can read other poems that involve animals. Poetry anthologies about animals include the following:
  - *Alphabeasts* by Dick King-Smith
  - *Pet Poems* by Jennifer Curry
  - *Alphabestiary: Animal Poems from A to Z* by Jane Yolen
  - *Monkeys Write Terrible Letters* by Arnold Spilka
  - *Animal Lullabies* by Pamela Conrad
  - *Animals on Parade* by Sara Willoughby Herb and Steve Herb

Name _____

Read the poem and answer the questions on the following pages.

Jojo is a monkey
Cute like an ape
A monkey for a pet?
What a huge mistake!

Our two daughters
So sweet and fair
Are missing great big
Clumps of hair!

Oh my goodness!
Jojo! STOP THAT!
You can't go riding
On the cat!

Boom! Bang! Crash!
Our home is a disaster!
Back to the pet shop
Faster! Faster!

Jojo we swapped
For a fish named Bubble.
He eats and swims
And is never any trouble.

JOJO THE MONKEY

Right There	Find the answers directly in the text.

1. Read each sentence. Choose the correct answer.

   a. How many daughters are there?

   ☐ one ☐ two ☐ three ☐ four

   b. Which word does *not* describe Jojo?

   ☐ cute ☐ naughty ☐ monkey ☐ calm

   c. What is the name of the fish?

   ☐ Cuddle ☐ Trouble ☐ Muddle ☐ Bubble

2. What are the daughters missing?

   _____

3. What did Jojo do to the cat?

   _____

Think and Search	Think about what the text says.

1. Where did Jojo the monkey come from? _____

2. Who do you think is "speaking" in the poem? _____

   Why do you think this? _____

   _____

3. How do you think the family was feeling when . . .

   a. they first brought Jojo home? _____

   b. Jojo was riding the cat? _____

   c. they brought Bubble home? _____

JOJO THE MONKEY

On Your Own   Use what you know about the text and your own experience.

1. Who would you rather have as a pet?   ☐ Jojo ☐ Bubble

Explain your choice. _____

_____

_____

2. "Jojo the Monkey" is a rhyming poem. The last words in line 2 and line 4 of each stanza rhyme (or almost rhyme).

For example:

Stanza 1:

Line 1	Jojo is a monkey	(doesn't rhyme)
Line 2	Cute like an **ape**	(rhymes)
Line 3	A monkey for a pet?	(doesn't rhyme)
Line 4	What a huge **mistake**!	(rhymes)

List the four other pairs of rhyming words in the poem.

- _____   _____

- _____   _____

- _____   _____

- _____   _____

3. What animal would you replace Jojo with? Give reasons why.

_____

_____

_____

_____

JOJO THE MONKEY

Synthesizing

Use the text on page 85 to help you complete the following activity. The family in the poem had a terrible time when they brought Jojo home from the pet shop. Imagine you have brought an unusual pet home to your house that causes a problem.

1. Plan a poem about this pet.

Type of animal: _____ Pet's name: _____

What does the pet do to make you take him or her back to the pet shop?

_____

_____

2. Write your poem. Make the words at the end of line 2 and line 4 rhyme.

Line 1 _____ is a _____

Line 2 _____ (rhyme)

Line 3 _____

Line 4 _____ (rhyme)

Line 1 _____

Line 2 _____ (rhyme)

Line 3 _____

Line 4 _____ (rhyme)

3. Draw a picture of your pet causing trouble.

_____

Genre: Report

READING FOCUS

- Analyzes and extracts information from a report to answer literal, inferential, and applied questions
- Scans a report to find relevant information to complete a fact file
- Uses synthesis to complete a fact file about an animal

ANSWER KEY

Right There (Page 91)

1. They fly high in the air, and they don't often come to the ground.

2. a. 3 months   b. 12 inches   c. 2 colored markings   d. 4 months

3. The pipe vine leaves have made it poisonous.

Think and Search (Page 91)

1. The length of the wings spread out from end to end.

2. To attract the female butterfly.

On Your Own (Page 92)

1. Answers will vary.   2. Drawings will vary.

Applying Strategies (Page 93)

a. Queen Alexandra's Birdwing butterfly

b. Males are smaller and have black wings with yellow, blue, green, and red markings. Females have dark brown wings with cream and red markings. Both have bright yellow bodies.

c. feed on nectar of flowers

d. rainforest in Papua New Guinea

e. adult female lays eggs, caterpillar hatches from the egg, cocoon, transforms into a butterfly

f. feeds on nectar and flies high in the air

g. It is endangered. Their habitat is being destroyed, and some people illegally catch and sell the butterflies for money.

h. butterfly farms, protecting areas of the rainforest, grow the pipe vine in different habitats

i. Answers will vary.

EXTENSIONS

- Students can collect other animal reports from the Internet or the library. Discuss the kind of information they contain.

GIANT BUTTERFLY

Name _____

Read the report and answer the questions on the following pages.

Do you know which is the largest butterfly in the world? It is the Queen Alexandra's Birdwing butterfly. The wingspan of the female butterfly can be up to 12 inches long. That's the length of a ruler!

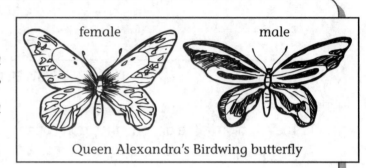

Queen Alexandra's Birdwing butterfly

This amazing animal lives in a small area of rainforest in Papua New Guinea. Like all butterflies, it begins life as an egg. The female Queen Alexandra's Birdwing lays eggs on only one type of plant—the pipe vine. It then takes four months for the whole transformation into a butterfly. First, a caterpillar hatches from the egg. The caterpillar then eats the leaves of the pipe vine until it is ready to make a cocoon. Inside the cocoon, it transforms into a butterfly. The Queen Alexandra's Birdwing butterfly usually lives for about three months. It is not often eaten by predators. One reason for this is that the pipe vine leaves eaten by the caterpillar are poisonous.

Male and female Queen Alexandra's Birdwings look different from each other. The males are smaller and have black wings with yellow, blue, green, and red markings. The females have dark brown wings with cream and red markings. Both the male and female butterflies have bright yellow bodies.

Queen Alexandra's Birdwings like to fly high in the air when they are not feeding on the nectar of flowers. They don't often come to the ground, so this can make getting an accurate count of how many exist difficult. But it is known that they are endangered. This is mainly because large areas of their rainforest home have been cleared of trees by people for farming and houses. Some people also catch and sell the butterflies for large sums of money, which is against the law.

The government of Papua New Guinea is trying to save the butterfly by helping people to set up butterfly farms, protecting areas of the rainforest from logging, and planning to grow the pipe vine in different habitats.

GIANT BUTTERFLY

Right There   Find the answers directly in the text.

1. What makes it difficult to find out how many Queen Alexandra's Birdwing butterflies there are?

_____

_____

2. Answer the following questions.

   a. For how many months does the adult butterfly live?

   _____

   b. How many inches long can the butterfly's wingspan be?

   _____

   c. How many different colored markings are found on the female butterfly's wings?

   _____

   d. How many months does the whole transformation take?

   _____

3. Why is the adult butterfly not often eaten by predators?

_____

_____

Think and Search   Think about what the text says.

1. What do you think is meant by the word *wingspan*?

_____

_____

2. What might be one reason the male butterfly is more brightly colored than the female?

_____

_____

GIANT BUTTERFLY

On Your Own   Use what you know about the text and your own experience.

1. Do you think catching and selling endangered
   animals should be illegal? Explain why/why not.

_____

_____

_____

_____

_____

_____

_____

_____

2. Create a poster to encourage people to save the Queen Alexandra's
   Birdwing butterfly.

GIANT BUTTERFLY

Scanning

Create a fact file using the information from the report on page 90.

Fact File

a. Name	**d.** Habitat
b. Appearance of adults	
	e. Stages of life cycle
c. What do the adults eat?	**f.** Adult habits

g. Problems for this animal

h. Suggested solutions

i. Do you think it is important to help this animal? Why or why not?

Genre: Newspaper Article

READING FOCUS

- Analyzes and extracts information from a newspaper article to answer literal, inferential, and applied questions

- Uses synthesis to imagine himself/herself in the role of a television reporter

- Uses prediction to write a television news story

ANSWER KEY

Right There (Page 96)

1. The "Soarosaurus" is a flying dinosaur with wings about the length of a bus and a body about the size of an elephant's.

2. They are too busy digging for more bones.

3. Answers should include three of the following: the archeologists have not yet shown the full skeleton; the photographs of the leg bones could be from a number of different dinosaurs; it is surprising that something the size of an elephant could fly; the team might want to become famous or make money; the photographs were very blurry.

Think and Search (Page 96)

1. a–b. Answers will vary.

2. Answers will vary.

On Your Own (Page 97)

Answers will vary.

Applying Strategies (Page 98)

1–4. Answers will vary.

EXTENSIONS

- Teacher can share articles from newspapers and the Internet. Use them as examples to help the students write their own articles.

- Students can research different types of dinosaurs.

- Students can search on the Internet for images of dinosaur bones displayed in museums.

Name _____

Read the newspaper article and answer the questions on the following pages.

Australian Dinosaur Claim

The remains of an unusual dinosaur may have been found in Australia——if a team of archeologists is to be believed.

The team claims to have found the complete skeleton of a flying dinosaur, which they have named "Soarosaurus."

"Our find will astound the world," said a member of the team yesterday. "The dinosaur is the most enormous animal that has ever flown. Its wings are about the length of a bus, and its body is the size of an elephant's."

Although the news of the find has many scientists buzzing with excitement, others are skeptical, saying, "they will believe it when they see it."

"The archaeologists have yet to show the full skeleton to the world," says Professor Kent Binnings of Carleton University. "So far, I have only seen photographs of a few leg bones, which could be from a number of different dinosaurs. I would be very surprised if something the size of an elephant could fly."

Well-known archeologist Sandra Green agrees, suggesting that the Australian team is either mistaken or playing some kind of joke. "The idea of this dinosaur existing is ridiculous," she says. "I suspect the team just wants to become famous or make money. The photographs of the dinosaur I was shown were very blurry and could have been of large bones of other animals."

The team has refused to show any more photographs, saying that they are too busy digging for more bones in the secret location where they claim the skeleton was found.

DINOSAUR FIND?

Right There   Find the answers directly in the text.

1. Describe the dinosaur the archeologists claim to have found.

_____

_____

2. Why does the team say it has not taken more photographs?

_____

_____

3. List three reasons why Binnings and Green find it hard to believe the archeologists.

- _____

- _____

- _____

Think and Search   Think about what the text says.

1. a. Choose another suitable name for the Soarosaurus.

_____

b. Explain why you chose this name.

_____

_____

2. Do you believe the archeologists? Why/Why not?

_____

_____

DINOSAUR FIND?

On Your Own   Use what you know about the text and your own experience.

Imagine that the world's most amazing dinosaur find happens tomorrow. Write a list of reasons why it is so amazing.

_____

_____

_____

_____

_____

_____

_____

_____

_____

_____

_____

_____

_____

_____

_____

_____

_____

DINOSAUR FIND?

Imagine you are a television news reporter. You read the article on page 95 and decide to find out if the archeologists are telling the truth. You discover the secret location and arrive there unnoticed.

1. Describe what you think you will see.

_____

_____

2. Before anyone notices you, write three questions to ask the team.

- _____

- _____

- _____

3. A member of the team figures out you are a reporter. She is angry but agrees to talk to you. Write what you think her answer will be for each of your questions.

- _____

_____

- _____

_____

- _____

4. You return to work to write a report for the news that night. Write the opening three or four sentences of your report below.

_____

_____

_____

_____

Genre: Diary

READING FOCUS

- Analyzes and extracts information from a diary entry to answer literal, inferential, and applied questions
- Summarizes information about a character from a diary entry
- Predicts a future diary entry for a character based on the information gained from an earlier entry

ANSWER KEY

Right There (Page 101)

1. hundreds

2. a. She knew that she would find plenty of crumbs and other tasty treats.

   b. The queen was ill, and the extra food would make her better.

   c. She was afraid of falling.

Think and Search (Page 101)

1. Answers will vary. Possible answer(s): the fabric is slippery, it sometimes has tricky folds.

2. Answers will vary. Possible answer(s): worst day ever, worried, panicked, scared, tired, lonely.

On Your Own (Page 102)

Drawings and answers will vary.

Applying Strategies (Page 103)

1. Some answers may vary. Possible answer(s):

   Home—rotten log

   Job—collect and bring food back to the colony for the queen ant

   Things she is good at/likes to do—knowing where to find food, thinking fast to get out of trouble, moving quickly

   Things she is not as good at/doesn't like to do—climbing up trousers and jeans

   Other details—Answers will vary.

2. Answers will vary.

EXTENSIONS

- Other suggested titles include the following:
  - *The Diary of a Young Roman Girl* by Moira Butterfield
  - *Penny Pollard's Diary* by Robin Klein
  - *Royal Diaries* series by various authors (Scholastic)

Name _____

Read the diary entry and answer the questions on the following pages.

Dear diary,

Today has been so terrifying I can hardly bring myself to write about it. It began like any other day. I woke up early and scurried off to meet the hundreds of other worker ants. When I arrived, they were talking about the queen.

"She is ill," I heard one of them say. "We need to find extra food today to help make her better."

I could hardly believe my antennae! Our queen, not well? This could mean disaster for the colony. Right away, I raced out of our rotten log home and into the picnic ground. I knew the best place to find food—under the picnic table. There were always lots of breadcrumbs and other tasty treats there.

I am usually very careful about watching where I am going, but today, I was thinking so hard about getting the food that I forgot to look out for our worst enemy—humans. Only when the sky went dark did I look up and realize that the sole of a human shoe was about to stomp on me.

I only had a split second to decide what to do. I couldn't stay on the ground, so I ran up the human's bare leg. I was glad that he was wearing shorts. Trousers and jeans are so difficult to race up quickly! I ran up to his knee and paused for a moment. I didn't want to go any higher—I was afraid of falling. I got so worried that before I knew it, I bit the human's leg.

"Ow!" His hand darted towards me. I gulped and just managed to duck out of the way.

"James! Time to go!"

The human started to walk, so I clung on as best I could, trying not to move. I knew that if he felt me, he would try to slap me again. He arrived at a car and got in. As soon as he slammed the door, the car started moving. I made my way onto the rough carpet, trembling and shaking. I hid under the front seat and stayed there until the car stopped moving and the humans got out.

Now I am stuck here! There is no food, and I don't know where I am. I'll have to find a way out tomorrow. Will I ever see home again?

Myrmecia

DIARY OF AN ANT

Right There   Find the answers directly in the text.

1. How many ants does Myrmecia work with? _____

_____

2. Answer the following questions.

   a. Why does Myrmecia head for the picnic table? _____

   _____

   b. Why did the worker ants need to find extra food? _____

   _____

   c. Why didn't Myrmecia want to climb too high? _____

   _____

Think and Search   Think about what the text says.

1. Why might it be difficult for an ant to run up trousers quickly?

_____

_____

_____

2. List four words or phrases to describe how Myrmecia
may have felt about her day.

   • _____

   • _____

   • _____

   • _____

DIARY OF AN ANT

On Your Own   Use what you know about the text and your own experience.

Imagine this diary entry is going to be made into the opening scenes of an animated movie. Draw three movie frames that show the most exciting parts of the diary entry. Add a caption next to each frame.

DIARY OF AN ANT

Use the text on page 100 to help you complete the following activities. Myrmecia's diary entry ends with her shut in the car. What do you think might happen to her the next day?

1. Begin by listing the information you have learned about her so far.

Home	Job
Things she is good at/likes to do	Things she is not as good at/doesn't like to do
Other details	

2. Use the information to write the first four to five sentences of Myrmecia's next diary entry.

Predicting

Dear diary, _____

_____

_____

_____

_____

_____

Genre: Folktale

READING FOCUS

- Analyzes and extracts information from a folktale to answer literal, inferential, and applied questions
- Creates a summary of a folktale by completing details of its setting, characters, and main events
- Scans a folktale to find relevant information about the setting, characters, and events
- Uses sensory imaging to draw imagined pictures of events contained in a folktale

---

ANSWER KEY

Right There (Page 106)

1. He gave most of what he had to others.

2. His farm was not doing well.

3. a. Answers will vary. Possible answer(s): she was so skinny her ribs stuck out; the man wanted to sell her at the market; Halvar swapped her for seven goats.

   b. Answers will vary. Possible answer(s): they appeared in the farmer's barn in place of the cow; they gave the man more milk than he could ever drink; they made the man very rich.

Think and Search (Page 106)

1. Answers will vary. Possible answer(s): They love to play in Halvar's house because they know the story of his kindness.

2. he felt too busy and important.

On Your Own (Page 107)

Answers will vary.

Applying Strategies (Page 108)

1. Answers will vary.

2. Halvar; opinions will vary.

   the man; opinions will vary.

3. 1 Halvar offered to help the man.

   2 The man opened his barn door.

   3 The goats made the man rich.

   4 The man saw Halvar again.

EXTENSIONS

- Collections of folktales from around the world can be found in the following books:
  - *Folktales and Fables* series by Robert Ingpen and Barbara Hayes
  - *Rich Man, Poor Man, Beggarman, Thief: Folk Tales From Around the World* by Marcus Crouch
  - *The Young Oxford Book of Folk Tales* by Kevin Crossley-Holland

HALVAR'S HOUSE

Name _____

Read the folktale from Sweden and answer the questions on the following pages.

Once there was a giant named Halvar. He lived in a huge stone house in the hills. Halvar was a very poor giant because he gave most of what he had to others. This made him happy.

One day, Halvar was sitting outside his house when a man came past, leading a cow. The man was wearing ragged clothes. The cow was so skinny that Halvar could see her ribs sticking out.

"Hello," the man called out to Halvar. "Can you tell me if this road leads to the markets?"

"Yes it does," said Halvar. "Are you hoping to sell your cow?"

"Yes," said the man. "Although I'm not too hopeful. You can see how thin she is. But I have no choice. My farm is not doing well, and I need to eat."

Halvar felt sorry for the man. "I would like to help you," he said. "Go home, and put your cow back in the barn. In the morning, you will find seven goats in her place."

The man could hardly believe his ears. But he had heard of Halvar's kindness and decided to take a chance. He walked back home and put the cow in the barn.

The next morning, the man opened the barn door to find seven goats instead of the cow. From that time on, life got much better for the man. The goats gave him more milk than he could ever drink. He made some of the milk into cheese and sold it for a good price at the market. Soon, the man became very rich and forgot all about Halvar. Then one day, he passed by Halvar's house again. This time, he was riding a beautiful horse.

"Hello," Halvar called out. "Come and chat with me for a while."

"I haven't got time," said the man. "Don't you know that I'm an important man in the village now?"

Sadly, Halvar watched the man ride away. But then he remembered how much he enjoyed giving things away and making people happy. He kept on being kind to others no matter how they treated him.

Today, Halvar's house still stands in the hills of Sweden. It is a place where children love to play.

HALVAR'S HOUSE

Right There   Find the answers directly in the text.

1. Why was Halvar poor?

   _____

   _____

2. Why was the man poor?

   _____

   _____

3. Write a fact about each animal from the story.

   a. cow _____

   b. goats _____

Think and Search   Think about what the text says.

1. Why do you think children might love to play in Halvar's house?

   _____

   _____

2. Choose the best ending for the sentence.

   The man didn't stop to talk to Halvar because

   ❑ he had a beautiful horse.

   ❑ he felt too busy and important.

   ❑ he didn't like Halvar.

   ❑ he didn't recognize Halvar.

HALVAR'S HOUSE

On Your Own   Use what you know about the text and your own experience.

Imagine the man had stopped to talk to Halvar. Write a new ending for the folktale.

The man got off his horse and spoke to Halvar. _____

_____

_____

_____

_____

_____

_____

_____

_____

_____

_____

_____

_____

_____

_____

_____

_____

_____

HALVAR'S HOUSE

Summarizing

Use the text on page 105 to help you complete the following activity. Write a summary of "Halvar's House" by completing the details below.

1. Setting
Describe what you think Halvar's house looks like.

_____

_____

2. Characters
Write the names of the two main characters in the story. Under each, write your opinion of the character's behavior in the story.

Character 1

_____

Opinion

_____

Character 2

_____

Opinion

_____

3. Main Events
Order the events below from 1 to 4. Draw a picture to show each event.

☐

The man opened his barn door.

☐

Halvar offered to help the man.

☐

The man saw Halvar again.

☐

The goats made the man rich.

 ©Teacher Created Resources

Standards Correlations

Each lesson meets one or more of the following Common Core State Standards © Copyright 2010. National Governors Association Center for Best Practices and Council of Chief State School Officers. All rights reserved. For more information about the Common Core State Standards, go to http://www.corestandards.org/ or http://www.teachercreated.com/standards.

Reading Literature/Fiction Text Standards	Text Title	Pages
Key Ideas and Details		
ELA.RL.3.1 Ask and answer questions to demonstrate understanding of a text, referring explicitly to the text as the basis for the answers.	The Amazing Adventure	9–13
	A DVD Dimension	14–18
	The Ant and the Dove	19–23
	King Arthur	24–28
	Gavin the Gentle Giant	29–33
	Cirrus the Centaur's Show	44–48
	Don't You Dare Tell	49–53
	The Marshes	54–58
	Remote Control	59–63
	The School Play	64–68
	April Fools!	79–83
	Jojo the Monkey	84–88
	Diary of an Ant	99–103
	Halvar's House	104–108
ELA.RL.3.2 Recount stories, including fables, folktales, and myths from diverse cultures; determine the central message, lesson, or moral and explain how it is conveyed through key details in the text.	The Ant and the Dove	19–23
	King Arthur	24–28
	Gavin the Gentle Giant	29–33
	Cirrus the Centaur's Show	44–48
	Halvar's House	104–108
ELA.RL.3.3 Describe characters in a story (e.g., their traits, motivations, or feelings) and explain how their actions contribute to the sequence of events.	The Amazing Adventure	9–13
	The Ant and the Dove	19–23
	King Arthur	24–28
	Gavin the Gentle Giant	29–33
	Cirrus the Centaur's Show	44–48
	Don't You Dare Tell	49–53
	The Marshes	54–58
	The School Play	64–68
	April Fools!	79–83
	Diary of an Ant	99–103
	Halvar's House	104–108

Common Core State Standards (cont.)

Reading Literature/Fiction Text Standards (cont.)	Text Title	Pages
Craft and Structure		
ELA.RL.3.4 Determine the meaning of words and phrases as they are used in a text, distinguishing literal from nonliteral language.	The Amazing Adventure The Ant and the Dove King Arthur Gavin the Gentle Giant Cirrus the Centaur's Show The Marshes Remote Control The School Play April Fools! Jojo the Monkey Diary of an Ant	9–13 19–23 24–28 29–33 44–48 54–58 59–63 64–68 79–83 84–88 99–103
ELA.RL.3.5 Refer to parts of stories, dramas, and poems when writing or speaking about a text, using terms such as chapter, scene, and stanza; describe how each successive part builds on earlier sections.	The School Play Jojo the Monkey	64–68 84–88
ELA.RL.3.6 Distinguish their own point of view from that of the narrator or those of the characters.	A DVD Dimension The Ant and the Dove King Arthur Gavin the Gentle Giant Don't You Dare Tell Remote Control The School Play April Fools!	14–18 19–23 24–28 29–33 49–53 59–63 64–68 79–83
Integration of Knowledge and Ideas		
ELA.RL.3.7 Explain how specific aspects of a text's illustrations contribute to what is conveyed by the words in a story (e.g., create mood, emphasize aspects of a character or setting).	King Arthur Cirrus the Centaur's Show Remote Control The School Play Jojo the Monkey	24–28 44–48 59–63 64–68 84–88

Common Core State Standards (cont.)

Reading Literature/Fiction Text Standards (cont.)	Text Title	Pages
Range of Reading and Level of Text Complexity		
ELA.RL.3.10 By the end of the year, read and comprehend literature, including stories, dramas, and poetry, at the high end of the grades 2–3 text complexity band independently and proficiently.	The Amazing Adventure	9–13
	A DVD Dimension	14–18
	The Ant and the Dove	19–23
	King Arthur	24–28
	Gavin the Gentle Giant	29–33
	Cirrus the Centaur's Show	44–48
	Don't You Dare Tell	49–53
	The Marshes	54–58
	Remote Control	59–63
	The School Play	64–68
	April Fools!	79–83
	Jojo the Monkey	84–88
	Diary of an Ant	99–103
	Halvar's House	104–108

Reading Informational Text/Nonfiction Standards	Text Title	Pages
Key Ideas and Details		
ELA.RI.3.1 Ask and answer questions to demonstrate understanding of a text, referring explicitly to the text as the basis for the answers.	Beatrix Potter	34–38
	Two Letters	39–43
	From the Cow to You	69–73
	How to Make Slime	74–78
	Giant Butterfly	89–93
	Dinosaur Find?	94–98
ELA.RI.3.2 Determine the main idea of a text; recount the key details and explain how they support the main idea.	Beatrix Potter	34–38
	From the Cow to You	69–73
	Giant Butterfly	89–93
	Dinosaur Find?	94–98
ELA.RI.3.3 Describe the relationship between a series of historical events, scientific ideas or concepts, or steps in technical procedures in a text, using language that pertains to time, sequence, and cause/effect.	From the Cow to You	69–73
	How to Make Slime	74–78
	Giant Butterfly	89–93

Reading Informational Text/Nonfiction Standards *(cont.)*	Text Title	Pages
Craft and Structure		
ELA.RI.3.4 Determine the meaning of general academic and domain-specific words and phrases in a text relevant to a *grade 3 topic or subject area.*	Beatrix Potter Two Letters From the Cow to You How to Make Slime Giant Butterfly Dinosaur Find?	34–38 39–43 69–73 74–78 89–93 94–98
ELA.RI.3.5 Use text features and search tools (e.g., key words, sidebars, hyperlinks) to locate information relevant to a given topic efficiently.	From the Cow to You How to Make Slime	69–73 74–78
ELA.RI.3.6 Distinguish their own point of view from that of the author of a text.	Giant Butterfly	89–93
Integration of Knowledge and Ideas		
ELA.RI.3.7 Use information gained from illustrations (e.g., maps, photographs) and the words in a text to demonstrate understanding of the text (e.g., where, when, why, and how key events occur).	Beatrix Potter Two Letters From the Cow to You How to Make Slime Giant Butterfly	34–38 39–43 69–73 74–78 89–93
ELA.RI.3.8 Describe the logical connection between particular sentences and paragraphs in a text (e.g., comparison, cause/effect, first/second/third in a sequence).	Two Letters From the Cow to You How to Make Slime Giant Butterfly	39–43 69–73 74–78 89–93
Range of Reading and Level of Text Complexity		
ELA.RI.3.10 By the end of the year, read and comprehend informational texts, including history/ social studies, science, and technical texts, at the high end of the grades 2–3 text complexity band independently and proficiently.	Beatrix Potter Two Letters From the Cow to You How to Make Slime Giant Butterfly Dinosaur Find?	34–38 39–43 69–73 74–78 89–93 94–98